The Education Bill of Rights

A Summary of Findings from the ABA Civil Rights and Social Justice Section's Education Focus Groups

Beth K. Whittenbury, J.D.

Library of Congress Control Number 2017953476

ISBN 10: 0-692-91768-3
ISBN-13: 978-0-692-91768-8

Published by the American Bar Association, Section of Civil Rights and Social Justice

Printed in the USA

FOREWORD

In 2009, the Education Committee of the Civil Rights and Social Justice Section ("CRSJ," then known as the Section of Individual Rights and Responsibilities) of the American Bar Association ("ABA"), launched an initiative to determine if citizens of the several states had any common agreement on the essential elements of a quality education and to see if most citizens agreed that a quality education is a fundamental right essential to the functioning of our democratic form of government. That initiative envisioned focus groups held around the country made of no more than ten individuals per group with each group comprised of the most diverse members possible: politically, racially, and socio-economically.

Surprisingly, the Committee found few willing to commit volunteer time to this endeavor in 2009, although one such focus group in the Los Angeles area finished the task that year. The results of that focus group were relayed as part of a Continuing Legal Education presentation at the 2009 ABA Annual Meeting entitled: "The Right to Quality Education in America: What is it? What Should it Look Like?"

In 2016, the CRSJ Education Committee revisited this project and joined forces with ABA President Linda Klein's Commission on the Lawyer's Role in Assuring Every Child's Right to a High-Quality Education ("Education Commission"). We set a deadline of June 30, 2017 for our results. By that date, we had received reports from twelve different focus groups from around the country. The individual reports from these groups can be found on the CRSJ Education Committee Website at http://apps.americanbar.org/dch/committee.cfm?com=IR504100. The groups developed as volunteers stepped in to lead them.

We would like to thank the lawyers, educators, and concerned citizens that took the time to meet and thoughtfully express their opinions on this important issue. The individuals engaging in these groups ranged in age from 18 to 71, and included members of most races and ethnicities. The education level of the participants ranged from a fourth grade level education to holders of PhDs. Both men and women participated with members of the LGBT community represented.

We purposefully gave loose instructions for the groups in order to leave open the field of discussion. We did not want to direct the findings in any way, but instead to honestly and openly encourage feedback from across the nation. As a result, the focus groups may not be considered control groups under traditional empirical research standards, but they have served to give clear, unbiased pictures showing points of agreement from around the country. Consequently, no two focus groups created identical categories or suggestions. Each used their own terminology in explaining what they felt were the essential elements of a quality education.

This approach challenged us when creating a useful summary of findings, but we feel it made the overall findings richer and more pointed than would have otherwise occurred. The following pages contain the results of our findings. Cumulatively, we have named these findings the "Education Bill of Rights" since the findings reflect what our focus groups from across the nation have determined to be the most essential elements of a high quality education.

The pearls of wisdom found within each focus group's write-ups did not always fit within broad categories. However, the author worked hard to incorporate these golden nuggets where possible. She hopes she has done justice to the time and effort spent by the focus groups when compiling this report. May this summary begin a broader discussion about realizing a right to a quality education. This book is intended to inspire and guide further work on behalf of our children and our society.

CONTENTS

ACKNOWLEDGMENTS

We would like to acknowledge Reggie Turner, Chair of the ABA Presidential Commission on the Lawyer's Role in Assuring Every Child's Right to a High-Quality Education for his help and support with this project, Aidan Browoleit, an aspiring law student, for his help collating this data in the summer of 2017, Michelle McCleod who put the first charts together collating this information, Melanie Browoleit for proofreading this book, and Paul Freese for his fact gathering for this project.

We would also like to thank the people who formed and ran our twelve focus groups including Garry Bevel of the Partnership for Child Health, Jennifer Marshall, William Whittenbury, Krista Galleberg, Ardath Hamann, Linda Britton, Reggie Turner, Valerie Hirschberg, Deshaud Brunson, Leslie Hayashi, and Ayan Islam.

THE EDUCATION BILL OF RIGHTS

When overlaid, the focus group results clearly showed points of agreement on the essential elements of a quality education. The following list comprises the Education Bill of Rights and each of these elements will be more thoroughly discussed in the subsequent chapters.

1. Proper Funding
2. Adequate Curriculum
3. Addressing the Needs of the Whole Child
4. Qualified Teachers
5. Proper Learning Environment
6. Alternatives to Traditional Education
7. Parental, Student, and Community Involvement
8. Restorative Justice Programs Rather than Traditional Discipline
9. Early, Pre-K Education
10. Supportive Administration

1 PROPER FUNDING

The main funding comments break down to the following categories:

1. Adequate sustained and equitable funding. (7 groups.)

The groups emphasized that equitable funding is not always equal. Poorer school districts may need more funds to make up for the lack of parent financial contributions to their children's education. The Chicago group highlighted that wealth disparity between districts is problematic. Hawaii mentioned a concern about proper funding for "high need" students who often get overlooked in "equal" funding scenarios. "High need" encompasses not only disabled and special needs students, but also gifted students as well. One group specifically called out a concern with a disparity of funding between high wealth and poorer school districts.

2. Teacher resources and pay need to receive increased funding. (7 groups.)

Groups made such comments as teachers are not given sufficient funding to handle class sizes. Teachers are not paid enough, and the lack of pay tends to attract less qualified teachers. Teachers often end up having to pay for supplies out of their own meager salaries. Please note that the federal tax code has a special deduction for teacher supplies, indicating that the federal government knows that teachers consistently reach into their own pockets to adequately fund their classrooms.

3. Teachers salaries should be increased, taking into account individual educational attainment, performance and proficiency targets, student and peer feedback, level of continuing education, and other qualitative markers.(6 groups.)

Rather than pay teachers more in general, the groups seemed to propose merit-based pay increases. They emphasized that they didn't want to judge teacher success just by how their students performed on standardized tests, but rather on how the teachers met the needs of each student. The groups did not advocate rewarding teachers who just "taught to the test." They did advocate for peer and student evaluations as part of the performance evaluation for teachers.

4. Every school should have the financial resources to provide all necessary tools and instructors to meet the educational needs of students and faculty. (4 groups.)

The federal movement to encourage no more than twenty students in a class for grades first through third has left many districts having to choose between accepting inadequate federal funding to accomplish this objective and foregoing federal aid but meeting their budgets with more students per teacher. Smaller class sizes need to be adequately funded or they will not be achieved.

5. Charter schools tend to defund traditional public schools and disproportionally, negatively affect poorer groups. (4 groups.)

Most groups which discussed charter schools did not like the concept and felt that charter schools had an overall negative effect on the public school system. The rest felt that that the funding formulas for charter schools needed revision. The anti-charter school sentiment seemed to rise out of the understanding that charter schools achieve higher test scores by selecting who to let in, thereby denying equal access to the charter school system and perpetuating the learning gap for those most in need of extra help and resources.

6. Schools should be given more freedom in decisions regarding the use of funds and should involve community input. (3 groups.)

Several groups felt that strict funding formulas tied the hands of school districts and acknowledged that different districts might have different needs depending on community concerns. They felt that districts should have the freedom to allocate funds where they made the most sense for that district. They also felt that funding should be based on "more than just test scores," advocating for the use of other factors such as health and wellness. One group commented that "flat funding" requires schools to do more with less.

7. Schools need sufficient funding to lower class sizes. (3 groups.)

Although this concept was touched on in the previous discussion of teacher funding, the concept merits its own category. Several groups appeared to advocate for lower class sizes and felt that funding needs to be increased to realize this goal.

8. For funding purposes, how well a school/district is performing should be evaluated by other factors such as health and wellness, SEL assessments, and academic growth. (3 groups.)

Determining whether a school district or individual school deserves funding and at what level requires criteria that takes into account a range of topics beyond just how its students perform on standardized tests. What issues are the districts or schools facing with respect to the communities which they serve? Where did the school or district start with respect to the measurements used? How far has it come?

For many schools, the nationwide standardized test topics don't relate to the most pressing needs of the students. To help students become well-educated members of society, we must first consider how to raise them from where they started. Not all children start in the same place in terms of advantages and disadvantages which come from the demographic make-up of the community into which they are born. It should be noted that the Evanston group, composed entirely of college students, felt that "standardized tests are still the best way to measure district performance, although they are not perfect. Scores are currently affected by the neighborhood's affluence and how much parents care. Schools should at least be evaluated based on a single national minimum standards test. States should be able to enact more stringent standards if they wish."

9. More funding is needed for higher education. (2 groups.)

One group called for community college to be completely free for those attending. Another stated that while college should not be entirely free, federal funds should be used to alleviate student debt.

10. Schools should receive federal funding. (1 group.)

Although only one group specifically advocated for federal funding, several discussed the concept of federal vs. state funding. Most opted for a combination of both. However, the Washington D.C. group found that federal funding made the federal government too involved in what it felt should be the sovereign role of the states. Hawaii's focus group gave a long and varied list of possible tax revenue sources.

2 ADEQUATE CURRICULUM

The focus groups identified different elements they thought constituted an adequate curriculum. The following lists those elements and how many focus groups identified each.

1. The ability to read at an eighth grade level or higher. (6 groups.)

The Los Angeles group elaborated that if it is determined that a child has fallen behind his or her expected grade level at any evaluation period prior to the end of each grade level, the educational institution should apply early intervention methods designed to advance the child toward his or her grade level expectations. Such academic evaluations should be performed no less than twice per school year, beginning no later than the start of first grade. Interventions could also commence on teacher recommendation.

The group had several recommendations for intervention strategies which would not require much, if any, additional funding. They suggested that one-on-one, peer to peer tutoring/mentoring could harness student strengths and raise self-esteem by allowing students proficient in one subject to help students struggling in that subject. That group also cautioned against limiting the opportunity to be a tutor to those proficient in all subjects. For example, those tutoring a student in math could receive tutoring in language.

These tutoring programs could draw on their own senior youth in the school, thus adding to school spirit. Student mentors could receive scholastic credit and a recognition award upon graduation in return for tutoring/mentoring. Tutoring/mentoring preparation could include a 4 hour training class with the principal, covering rules of conduct, emergency response, etc.

The Los Angeles group also suggested senior adult to child tutoring/mentoring. By establishing a School Mentor Corps, schools could access a steady stream of youth and senior adult tutors/mentors via a volunteer and scholastic credit program. For security purposes, each tutor/mentor should be checked by Megan's law lists; finger printed and photographed. The program could access senior adults by means of a referral network among the families at the school, public advertisement, and utilizing already known retired professionals from the school system.

They recommended that once a week each child meet with his other tutor simply to be affirmed and encouraged in any academic concept and/or challenging element in his or her school/life experience. They also suggested a big brother/sister program in order to minimize the need for intervention.

The St. Louis focus group suggested that students be able to read at a tenth grade level. Whereas Chicago recommended "strong" reading skills and Evanston suggested reading proficiency, Evanston advocated for national reading, writing and speaking proficiency standards. Detroit felt there should be accountability for children to learn to read by 4th grade.

2. The ability to execute basic mathematical tasks. (5 groups.)

Evanston felt that Algebra II level math was all that should be required of high school students, but that they should have the option to take more and higher levels if they aspire to careers that will need such higher math skills. However, Los Angeles felt that basic math skills were enough. That group defined basic math skills as:

a. Addition and subtraction
b. Multiplication and long division
c. Use and manipulation of fractions (add/subtract, multiply/divide, reduce, etc.)

d. Use and manipulation of percentages (similar to "c" directly above)
e. Basic applied geometry (shapes, angles, distances)
f. Basic statistical analysis. (averages, means, medians, etc.)

St. Louis advocated for basic arithmetic and algebra skills.

3. Basic accounting skills and economic knowledge. (5 groups.)

St. Louis noted that proficiency in financial literacy is important. They were joined by other groups which enumerated such things as the ability to balance a checkbook, creating and maintaining a budget, and using a calculator or equivalent. Groups also noted the need to understand the effects of leverage, interest rates, and compounding as well as basic macroeconomics: national debt/deficit, GDP, balance of trade, tariffs, free-trade, cost of labor, and the importance of education when competing in the labor markets.

4. Exposure to personal care strategies. (5 groups.)

Under this heading, groups emphasized that education in such things such as consequences in decision-making, nutrition, health, interpersonal relationships, home economics, stress management, mental health care, exercise, and how to make proper choices are most important. One group further elaborated that learning to control impulsivity and to take personal responsibility are important for students.

Hawaii called for teaching students to embrace the "common good," a civic mission, and service learning through involvement in the community, as well as to be informed citizens.

5. Basic English grammar and writing skills. (5 groups.)

This category included suggestions such as:

a. The ability to define and use basic sentence structure.
b. The ability to write a coherent paragraph with a topic sentence.
c. The ability to write a business letter.

d. The ability to write a basic essay with a thesis sentence and concluding paragraph.
e. The ability to spell or use spell check.
f. The difference between different forms of words which sound the same (e.g. too, two, to).

6. Science and Technology. (4 groups.)

Although STEM or STEAM subjects are gaining much attention in the national discourse, only four of our twelve groups specifically mentioned such classes as necessary to a quality education. This fact may not indicate a disagreement by all groups on the importance of STEM education, but rather those groups failing to mention it may have felt other areas such as basic math and reading skills were more important.

The science and technology subjects discussed as important included:

a. The principles of momentum, inertia, gravity and other forces.
b. The earth relative to the solar system, galaxy and universe.
c. Basic chemical reactions.
d. Different sources of energy and how they are created.
e. Physical Earth Science in terms of avoiding or understanding the potential for natural disasters.
f. Graphical communications.
g. Keyboarding skills.
h. The ability to navigate the internet.

7. The ability to communicate and cooperate effectively with others. (4 groups.)

Palos Verdes enumerated the following as items that should be taught under this category:

a. Listening skills.
b. Public speaking.
c. Debate and reasoning skills.
d. Conflict resolution skills.
e. Personal responsibility.
f. Ethics.
g. Character development.

h. Etiquette/manners.

8. Vocational and extracurricular opportunities. (4 groups.)

The groups acknowledged that not all students may be college bound. At least for the time being, our society still needs skilled labor. Therefore, such skills should be taught, and students should have the opportunity to learn such skills with a mind to making a career out of those for which they show an affinity. Still, schools seem to cut such training from their offerings, leaving no opportunities for students to explore these career paths and talents. The groups that addressed this issue felt that schools should not just be college preparatory organizations, but rather institutions which prepare students to enter the workforce and contribute to society.

The groups also felt that extracurricular offerings helped students to stay engaged in school and perhaps opened up other avenues for students to explore with respect to their talents. Training in the arts fell into this category.

9. US and world history/geography. (3 groups.)

Los Angeles recommend teaching history in order to demonstrate to students elements such as cause-and-effect, consequences, and conflict resolution through real-world examples. To achieve this goal, they would not necessarily encourage students to memorize volumes of historical dates, names and facts, but more importantly, focus students on gaining functional wisdom and knowledge designed to equip them to make informed social/political decisions, elect representatives, and utilize the electoral process in the best interest of our country. .Examples of such lessons would include, but are not limited to:

a. Why our Civil War and the two World Wars were fought.
b. What caused changes within certain countries' political systems.
c. Major social, technological or economic progressions that drastically changed society and how they changed it. (Industrial Revolution, Internet, etc.)

With respect to geography, they took a similar tack, feeling that students need to know such things as:

a. The locations, names and capitals of each US state.
b. The continents and large demographic areas within them (i.e., Europe, Middle East, Asia).
c. Trading partners.
d. Raw materials, industries, or technologies indigenous to certain regions (diamonds, coal, oil, etc.).

Evanston pointed out that "There is currently a strong bias in favor of western history in curricula. This causes wide-spread ignorance of the causes of current geopolitical problems. Curricula also needs to be honest about mistakes made throughout US History rather than "sweeping them under a rug." Rather than offering World History, European History, and US History, schools should offer a two class sequence, one on Eastern History (including Africa) and one on Western History (including the US). Both classes should focus on the origins of current events. Hand-in-hand with this, schools should offer more non-western languages as part of their foreign language curriculum.

10. An understanding of the US government and judicial system (civics). (3 groups.)

Although listed last, this point is arguably the most important to perpetuating our form of government in the United States. If students do not have an understanding of this subject, our democracy will not function well. Students will not understand the importance of casting informed votes in elections, nor will they understand the repercussions of failing to vote or casting an ill-informed vote in any election.

The Education Commission and the CRSJ Education Committee proposed a resolution on this point to the ABA at the 2017 ABA Annual meeting. Now that the resolution has passed the ABA House of Delegate and become ABA policy, we hope that schools follow our lead in requiring such curriculum.[1]

Some of the specific topics for schools to consider teaching under this category are:

a. State vs. federal governments.
b. Constitution, statutes and common law.

---

[1]The text of the resolution and accompanying report can be found at Appendix M at the back of this book.

c. The electoral process and the role of elected officials.
d. How do judges get/keep their jobs and what is their job?
e. Civil vs. criminal actions.
f. The role of regulations and how they are created.
g. The balance of powers.
h. What is a democracy and why is it our choice?
i. Other types of governments and how they differ from ours.

Other Thoughts on Curriculum

The St. Louis Group raised some additional points about curriculum. They felt curriculum should not be centered on standardized testing but rather holistic evaluation of education. There should be a skeletal national curriculum that ensures minimum academic standards are attainable. Schools and teachers should, however, have ownership and flexibility in developing curriculum to meet these academic standards.

3 ADDRESSING THE NEEDS OF THE WHOLE CHILD

The Jacksonville focus group most eloquently summed up this component of the Education Bill of Rights.

"Education does not exist in a vacuum. Neither are the experiences of students, faculty or staff isolated from their personal lives."

Eight of the focus groups discussed, in some aspect, addressing the needs of the whole child. These comments fell under the following categories.

1. Health Services. (6 groups.)

The Jacksonville group felt that like colleges, schools should be one-stop shops: medical, mental health, dentists, and necessary goods should be available on-site, including, where necessary, access to child care. Other groups agreed that quality healthcare (physical and mental) should be available for all in schools. Another group spoke in terms of "Wrap-Around" services including funding or support from NGOs to address those needs. Still others discussed the need for emotional and psychological support to be available on campus, advocating for at least a nurse, social worker, and school counselor in every school building.

2. After School Care. (2 Groups.)

Two groups called for after school care for younger students.

3. Other Thoughts on The Whole Child

The Hawaii focus group uniquely requested "Whole child education that includes global competencies." Oklahoma stated that, "Schools should provide multiple pathways to 'success,' meeting the needs of the entire spectrum of learners." Dallas asks for schools to recognize and elevate the talents of all children, use teaching techniques designed to match learning styles, use interest to "light the fire," provide opportunities for kids to move forward at their own pace, and offer a variety of teaching methods.

So many focus groups discussed a preference for restorative justice techniques as opposed to formal discipline that this sentiment became one of the ten components of the Education Bill of Rights. However, within the focus group reports, the topic of restorative justice was often discussed under the heading of addressing the needs of the whole child. Since restorative justice practices has become a component of the overall Bill of Rights, that concept will be discussed more fully in chapter eight.

4 QUALIFIED TEACHERS

Eight of the focus groups specifically mentioned quality teachers as an essential element of a quality education. Their comments in this regard break down to the following seven categories.

1. Extensive credentials and training. (5 groups.)

One group stated that, like doctors and lawyers, teachers should be licensed and have minimum continuing education requirements. Teacher education should include child socio-emotional development, classroom management techniques, childhood development, etc. First year teachers should receive extra support and training for their first year. Part of this support can come from other, more seasoned teachers who can provide models for others to emulate and follow. Great teachers should act as mentors and role models for all other teachers.

One group suggested creating a national standard of teacher quality. That group wanted to see the best state level teacher-training program adopted as a national standard. Other groups spoke in terms of wanting consistent and timely professional development for teachers. One group felt that teachers must be trained and qualified in specific content. Still another spoke of the need to recruit teachers from outside their geographic location. When these teachers relocate for a position they should find support adapting to their new environment and in making the transition to their new home.

2. Attentiveness to individual student needs. (5 groups.)

Teachers need to be trained to properly handle students with learning disabilities. One group specifically stated, "Students with disabilities have a right to teachers that have specific credentials and training in special education." Another focus group expanded this concept, calling for teachers who are trained in sensitivity to a broad range of student needs. Orlando pointed out that students with disabilities need to have a better support system and well-trained teachers. That group specified that students with disabilities should be able to reach basic literacy levels when they graduate high school.

3. Passion and engagement. (4 groups.)

This point resonated with multiple focus groups which called for teachers who are both motivated and capable/competent. Students need teachers who, themselves, have an ongoing commitment to learn and change as needed. Overall, the groups wanted teachers who are open to continuous learning.

4. Teachers who don't just teach to the test. (4 groups.)

The prevailing sentiment here was that students need truly dedicated teachers who guide pupils to be better thinkers and not just teach to the test.

5. Manageable class sizes. (3 groups.)

Several groups specifically called for smaller classrooms and fewer students per teacher. St. Louis advocated for classes of no more than twenty students. That group deemed a class size larger than twenty to be "realistically unmanageable and, therefore, inevitably unequal."

6. Teachers with cultural literacy. (3 groups.)

For this category the group uniformly felt that teachers and staff should have completed cultural diversity training and know how to effectively incorporate the positive elements of diversity into their classrooms.

7. Teachers need the right type and amount of resources to support them. (3 groups.)

The groups felt that teachers need the proper supplies to support their teaching curriculum and the proper resources with which to run their classrooms. Teachers also need the proper facilities and tools with which to do their jobs. The Orlando group quoted one its members, Deshaud Brunson, who said, "The great educators have to pay for their own materials, my great grandmother was an educator in the 1950's & 60's who, like most educators in the public schools today, paid for her own teaching material." Hawaii argued for an array of support for teachers from the community. The groups also felt that teachers should be paid based on performance and rewarded for innovation.

Finally, Evanston articulated what most groups implied, that teachers currently face a lack of prestige for their chosen profession. If they were paid in proportion to the importance of their job and given the proper support in terms of resources and training, this situation could change.

5 PROPER LEARNING ENVIRONMENT

Together, the groups listed a plethora of things that can create a conducive learning environment. These criteria break down into the following categories.

1. Students should have their basic needs met at school. (4 Groups.)

Most groups appeared to agree that students need clean and comfortable environments in which to learn. One group further broke down the basics needs of students into the following list of necessities:

- No mold or other hazards
- Clean/fresh air
- Potable drinking water
- Sanitary bathrooms and lunchrooms.

Although these things seem obvious, experience shows these basic necessities are not standard in all learning environments.

Of course, since children don't learn well on empty stomachs, schools should provide nutritional meals to students. One group specifically called for free nutritional breakfasts and lunches for all students.

2. Students need safety and security. (4 Groups.)

The groups also called for the safety and security of students on campus, as well as to and from school, which would include addressing bullying, drugs, discrimination, and violence. The Detroit group felt that research-based, state of the art systems should be available to protect the school environment. Where discipline is warranted, several groups felt that schools should use discipline programs designed to be fair and to rehabilitate, not simply to punish.

3. Schools need to provide adequate supplies, after school care/study space. (3 Groups.)

According to one group, children must have at least one hour per day to do their homework in a safe space with adequate supplies (e.g. computers, pencils, paper, tutors) and adult supervision. Another group argued for a minimum standard of school supplies and resources including up-to-date computers, textbooks, white boards, and any necessary instructional equipment along with free afterschool care which provides time for homework, games, and snacks).

4. Students need both physical and mental stimulation. (3 Groups.)

The concept of employing a social-emotional learning curriculum also came up in this context. One focus group's members agreed that students should have access to a diverse and integrated classroom environment, as they agreed there were many benefits to racial and socioeconomic integration in classroom settings.

St. Louis felt it important for students to have access to outdoor recreation and sports events. Hawaii felt students need curriculum that challenges and engages them.

6 ALTERNATIVES TO TRADITIONAL EDUCATION

Many of the groups felt it essential to offer vocational training in schools. Most acknowledged that not all students are college bound. Their comments in this respect are delineated below.

One group spent considerable time on this topic in their report. That group felt there is a general failure to recognize that not all students can or want to go to college. They felt there should be different paths through high school and that high schools are too focused on college preparation without recognition of technical paths. They noted that U.S. manufacturing requires specialized skills and that unskilled work has generally moved overseas. Automated manufacturing requires specialized training in technical systems. If these skills are not taught in schools, our country will not have people to fill these new domestic jobs.

Another group advocated for multiple tracks for students. They believe that educational institutions should provide optional skilled labor educational opportunities in addition to the required traditional academic education. That group suggests that the determination as to whether a student should participate in the alternative education program should be made collaboratively between the student, the parental guardian(s), and the educational staff. The objective of offering alternative opportunities is to allow the student to choose the educational path which best maximizes his or her overall future well-being, self-satisfaction, and long-term productive assimilation into society.

That group also recommends that students who choose to participate in the alternative education program be given a modified 'academic' curriculum to account for time and resources allocated to alternative education. That group sees that the most important forms of alternative education are vocational shops and apprenticeships where students learn both practical and marketable skills and trades.

If possible, students should be paid for doing productive work in order to discourage pupils from dropping out of school to pursue low-wage alternatives. A paid apprenticeship allows the student to develop professional skills, making them more marketable in society, and, at the same time, allows the student to stay in school to attain a traditional academic education.

Another group pointed out the importance of championing vocational training and opportunities so as to avoid preferencing collegiate tracks or influencing students away from gaining necessary vocational skills. That group believes education should be responsive to the needs and abilities of the individual students and should include vocational tracks and alternatives to standardized education that is strengths-based and purposeful. They believe this approach would help counter-balance current trends to teach to tests.

A different group advocated that students should have the opportunity to take a vocational track starting in tenth grade. This sentiment was mirrored by another group suggesting that students in grades eleven and twelve should have access to separate tracks: academic and vocational.

7 PARENTAL, STUDENT AND COMMUNITY INVOLVEMENT

The groups found parental, student and community involvement essential to a quality education.

1. Parent-School Collaboration. (6 groups.)

The Detroit group stated that: "parental involvement is essential; and schools must address the needs of parents in order to educate the children." Another group listed parent engagement as an important element of a quality education. The Dallas group wanted "a system that recognizes criticality of family involvement and support, and finds ways to engage that or provides alternatives." The Los Angeles Group made the following more lengthy comments.

The educational institution should encourage parental participation in the student's educational experience. This includes actively recruiting and encouraging parents to participate in PTA meetings, co-op programs, and field trips. The administration should urge parents to communicate regularly with teachers and school administrators, especially concerning sub-par homework or test performance, behavior problems, or emotional problems. The administration should work collaboratively with other community organizations such churches, athletic leagues, relevant governmental agencies and truancy programs to encourage parental participation. Where the teacher or administration feels a child is truly at risk, such teachers and/or administrators should feel free to visit the parents if they cannot get the parents to come to them.

2. Community Involvement. (7 Groups.)

The Dallas group called for an educational system that is transparent to parents and the community (its owners). They wanted an education system that is accountable to the community for desirable results. Los Angeles suggested the establishment of a National Corp of Senior Mentors to provide guidance, support, and tutoring to those students who lack family support. To that end, they encouraged the development of guidelines for teacher certification which would open doors for individuals to change careers and teach what they have been doing for many years in practice.

Hawaii suggested that non-profits could help provide funding for schools or specific programs within schools. For Hawaii, the idea of community-based education was a necessary component when creating a quality education for all. They felt that, although communities differ, resources for parents such as literacy programs, job resources, and second language learning should be included within the educational system. They recommended that each community should conduct a needs assessment. and then establish curriculum and programs to meet those needs. They also recommended fostering partnerships with community resources for schools as well as creating schools which actively involve and engage their communities.

Jacksonville suggested engaging frameworks (and/or marketing/PR professionals) to develop strategies to understand how the community thinks about public education. The entire community should then use these new frames, metaphors and shared values statements to reframe the discussion about education, thereby developing optimal delivery systems, positive environments (including the way discipline is handled), and measures of success. They also supported development of public-private partnerships to increase funding for schools, economic development in surrounding school communities, and offer students opportunities for professional internships and apprenticeships (for example, banking, law, medicine, aeronautics, nursing, cosmetology).

Oklahoma recommended utilizing a community school-based system that would meet the needs of that particular student body/community and decrease the one-size-fits-all-school requirements. They further suggested that schools partner with community resources (e.g. health care, mental health, food pantries, etc.) to meet identified needs. Like Hawaii, Oklahoma felt that schools should reflect the cultures of the communities which they serve. They also suggested that districts promote collaboration with systems of influence in the community.

Orlando stressed that the first priority of our education dollars should be the growth and development of our society. Palos Verdes thought that the schools should reach out to the community for volunteers who can come in and help schools meet minimum standards.

3. Student Involvement. (6 Groups.)

Hawaii felt that students should be actively engaged in their education. That group found it critical that students play an important role in describing their needs. To that end, they felt students should be allowed to take ownership of their education by having a say in the curriculum they take. They felt providing students these choices would help all pupils to develop a stake in their education.

Jacksonville somewhat mirrored those thoughts by stating that age-appropriate student feedback and input into the environment, curriculum, teacher performance, policies, and functioning of the school environment is critical to creating a sense of ownership and belonging for students. Oklahoma also felt that student needs should drive policy and approach. They felt that promoting an accountability system within the student body would help recognize the positive power of group influence. They also recommended inviting former students back into the school to offer internships and provide mentorships. The group remarked that students know what they need; educators need to be willing to ask, listen, and respond to students.

Palos Verdes felt that students should be given the opportunity to choose their own track (vocational vs. academic) in tenth grade. Chicago agreed that there should be two paths for students in high school, recognizing that not all students are college bound. Los Angeles suggested programs for students to assist each other through one-on-one, peer-to-peer tutoring and mentoring.

8 RESORATIVE JUSTICE PROGRAMS RATHER THAN TRADITIONAL DISCIPLINE

The ABA has done much work to curtail the school-to-prison pipeline. So, the fact that several of our focus groups, which pulled from many people outside of the ABA, mentioned the concept of restorative justice programs rather than traditional discipline is illustrative of the need to transition to this type of disciplinary approach in schools. In brief, restorative justice is a process which brings together persons harmed with persons responsible for harm in a safe and respectful space, promoting dialogue, accountability, and a stronger sense of community.[2] When used effectively, it can obviate the need for traditional discipline in most school contexts.

A full discussion of how to implement restorative justice programs in schools is beyond the scope of this chapter, but references to aid the reader in further research and understanding of these techniques are listed in the bibliography found at the end of this book. This chapter will summarize what our groups had to say about discipline in schools as an aspect of a fundamental right to a quality education.

Detroit summarized the groups feelings on this issue:

[2] Fania E. Davis, 8 Tips for Schools Interested in Restorative Justice, found at https://www.edutopia.org/blog/restorative-justice-tips-for-schools-fania-davis. Last visited 7/30/2017.

"Discipline programs must be fair, and designed to rehabilitate, not simply to punish. Excessive time out of school feeds the prison pipeline." In making this statement, the group was referring to the overwhelming use of suspensions and expulsions to address disciplinary problems in schools. Oklahoma echoed Detroit when it said, "Restorative Justice should be used as a framework for correcting student misconduct, limiting out-of-classroom time to address behaviors."

Jacksonville called for schools to institute Positive Behavioral Interventions and Support (PBIS) which focus on changing environments instead of the person. That group also advocated for a rights/equity based disciplinary system in schools. Los Angeles felt that instating a big brother/sister program would help limit the need for negative interventions.

9 EARLY, PRE-K EDUCATION

Several focus groups felt that early childhood education was essential to a quality education overall. However, they differed on when they felt such pre-K education should start and about the sources of funding for it.

One group felt that pre-K education starting at age four should be optional, but free if chosen. Another believed that every child should have an early learning foundation and that parents should be encouraged to engage their children in early childhood education.

Another group felt so strongly that its ten members unanimously agreed that a quality education must start at birth and continue through adulthood. They stated that the scientific evidence of the importance of early childhood education is overwhelming. Therefore, they felt that the need to foster community centers of learning at schools for all ages is critical to promoting a quality education.

Please note that a member of the Evanston group felt that two years of college level education should be mandatory.

10 SUPPORTIVE ADMINISTRATION

The groups determined that district and school administrations need to support both teachers as well as students, parents, and community interests in order for a quality education to thrive. Hawaii stated that: "Administrators (principals) need to be trained as both managers and leaders; they need to be visible/seen." Another group commented that the principals create the climate of the schools.

1. Administrative support for teachers.

Administrators need to support teachers by backing up discipline decisions and providing the resources teachers need to do their job. Administrators need to support innovations in the classroom instead of quashing them. They need to provide consistent mentorship. They also need to reward successful innovations, publicizing examples and working to incorporate them into other classrooms where warranted. Where administrators delegate to teachers, they need to do so effectively. Finally, they need to provide teachers meaningful evaluations.

2. Administrative support for students.

As mentioned previously, administrators need to work to keep children in school rather than jump to suspension and expulsion as the go-to disciplinary measure they apply. They also need to be cognizant of the whole child, getting to know each child's back-story and potential. They also need to be culturally aware, embracing and encouraging diversity. Most importantly, they need to be fair and equitable to all students.

3. Administrative support for parents.

Administrators should communicate well and often with parents, treating them as partners, not adversaries with respect to students interests. One group suggested that schools should provide parenting classes.

4. Administrative support for community.

Administrators should make an effort to identify and address community concerns. They should also make the school an integrated part of the community, endeavoring to meet community needs when possible and potentially providing continuing education opportunities for students, parents, and seniors in the community.

APPENDIX

In this section, we reproduce all the focus group reports. We do so in alphabetical order, not the order in which we received the reports. They have been reproduced just as we received them without edits of any kind. Appendix M contains the substance of the ABA resolution and report referenced in Chapter 2.

APPENDIX A – CHICAGO, IL

Memorandum

To: Beth Whittenbury
Co-chair, Public Education Committee
Individual Rights and Responsibilities Section

From: Ardath Hamann, Associate Professor, John Marshall Law School - Chicago

Date: May 24, 2017

Re: Chicago Focus Group on Right to Quality Education

What is important in education?
- Awareness of wider world
    - o Shouldn't be parochial or isolated
    - o Cultural awareness (e.g. geography is mostly US)
- Belief in every child's capacity to excel
- Strong Reading skills
- Children should have experience with children from a variety of backgrounds
- Quality v Minimum standards
- Specialization
- Broad humanities
- Life skills
    - o Vocation
    - o Budgeting

What makes a good teacher?
- Passion
- Ability to bring out a student's natural curiosity

- Bring subject alive
- Flexibility
- Individual attention
- Bring in original texts, maps
- Motivate kids to succeed
- Toughness
- High standards
- Listen to student
- Can't measure it by a test

Teachers need support (funding issue – below)
- Chicago Public Schools have 30-35/class
- Principals create the climate

Current education funnels toward test outcomes
- In comes (what are we giving to children) not out comes (test scores)
- Encourage curiosity not teach to test
- Standardized tests have become ceiling not floor

Funding
- Wide disparity among school districts
- Goal: free Community College (see Tennessee)
- Illinois not in position to increase school funding to equalize
- No solution on horizon

Failure to recognize that not all students can or want to go to college.
There should be different paths through HS
- High schools are too focused on college preparation
- No recognition of technical paths
    - o (e.g. BMW repair)
- U.S. manufacturing requires specialized skills
    - o unskilled work has moved overseas

o Automated manufacturing requires training in systems

Barriers to learning
- Not all children enter school equally ready to learn
- Family teaching is essential
- ESL barrier

Charters are not the solution
- They don't take time to figure out child
- They deal with all children in same manner
    - o If the child doesn't fit – left behind
- Few are more than moneymakers

Demographic information:
5 women/4 men
8 Caucasians/1 African-American
Age range: 28 - 70
Professions:
law professor
lawyer
IT specialist
home health aide
secretary
fundraiser
social worker
retired businessman
student

APPENDIX B – DALLAS, TX

ABA Civil Rights and Social Justice Section Education Committee Focus Group Dallas, Texas January 31, 2017

Organizers:

Linda Britton, Director, ABA Commission on Youth at Risk

Stephanie Hirsh, Executive Director, Learning Forward

Members of the focus group:

Karri Armstrong, Administrator, Republic Title Company

Meyer Denn, Executive Director, Center for Jewish Education

Tim Griffy – Retired Partner, Ernst & Young

H. Lynn Hadnot, Director, Collin County Juvenile Services, McKinney, Texas

Bobby Hillman, Special Education Teacher, Plano Independent School District, Plano, TX

Jo Ann H. Hill, Partner Ecosystem Leader, Education & Healthcare Markets, IBM

Sofia Rangal, Graduate, Texas Women's University, pending Texas teacher certification exam, working as a special education teaching assistant, Plano ISD, Plano, TX

Claudia Rotariu, Aesthetician

Joe Zarrehparvar, Chief Executive Officer, Wicresoft International

> *"Today knowledge [education] has power. It controls accessto opportunity and advancement."*
>
> Peter F. Drucker

About the Focus Group

Linda, Stephanie and their colleagues identified potential members of the focus group, making efforts to locate a diverse group of individuals that care about public education. Diversity is reflected in age, national origin, ethnicity, and gender, and includes immigrants to the US. A number of members are the first in their family to enter and complete college; two individuals state they are the youngest among many siblings to complete college, and another had missteps as a youth but was able to change the trajectory of his life by finishing high school and then college. Another completed college as a single parent. Many are parents of children, who now range in age from 4 years to adults. Almost all serve their communities as education-related volunteers, for example, as a board member of Texas Can Academy, as a leader of a faith-based initiative that serves economically-challenged students in Title 1 schools, as the spouse of a school board member, or as a STEM mentor for students.

At the beginning of the session, members reviewed a list of over 25 quotes about education and selected one to which he or she felt a connection. These quotes are included throughout the report. And, one member, who emigrated to the US from Romania, very wisely said, "all [of these quotes] mean the same thing to me; how important a teacher is, and how in a Communist country they want to give you little crumbs, while those at the top know everything."

> *"When I was a boy on the Mississippi River there was a proposition in a township there to discontinue public schools because they were too expensive. An old farmer spoke up and said if they stopped building the schools they would not save anything, because every time a school was closed a jail had to be built."*
>
> Mark Twain

A Constitutional Right to Education and its purpose

Members reviewed two articles, "An Overview of the History of Public Education in Texas", Texas Education Agency, and Stephen Lurie, "Why Doesn't the Constitution Guarantee the Right to Education?" The Atlantic, (Oct. 16, 2013). They raised these points of concern:

1. The rise in population growth in Texas does not correspond with the flat funding provided for public education. Texas schools must increasingly do more with less.
2. How can the United States allow itself to be 17th in the world in a ranking of educational systems? How do we allow our country to leave children behind?
3. Why do we not apply what happens in the rest of the world when we look at education in the US? Where are the lessons?
4. We have the money to spend on education, but we prioritize it differently. The Organization for

Economic Co-operation and Development (OECD) studies show that, in many countries, there is greater investment in preschool education and that investment brings bigger rewards.

5. Other countries that rank higher than the US are diverse as well and have many of the same problems as the US. They prioritize education higher than the US.
6. Why isn't there a constitutional amendment supporting a right to education? The limitations on providing equality in education are obvious and the 14th Amendment can only do so much.

> *"Education is not the filling of a pail, but the lighting of a fire."*
>
> William Butler

What are the goals and elements of a quality public education?

Each member wrote down 5 goals and 5 elements of a quality public education. The group split into two by gender; the male members then organized and prioritized the goals and the female members organized and prioritized the elements. The primary goal was to ensure the US position in the top ten of the world's education systems. Other goals included: to measure student abilities, to develop character, to embrace diversified learners, to create flexible systems for all learners, to ensure students are culturally and globally aware, and to educate all students regardless of age, gender, race, ethnicity or national origin, gender orientation, religion, or economic status. Attributes of each goal were included. The elements of a quality public school education were divided by administration, curriculum, teachers, and essential characteristics, and included attributes for each element. All of this information was put into the tables below:

Goals of a Quality Public Education	
National Goals	❖ Top 10 educational system in the world. Make it a goal like putting a man on the moon.
Measurable Student Abilities	❖ To allow each person the opportunity for growth and success (happiness) ❖ To lead a meaningful and productive life ❖ Learn a vocation ❖ Ability to understand numbers and finance ❖ Know how to communicate ❖ Ability to express oneself verbally and in writing ❖ Read and write ❖ Know how to study
Character Development	❖ Learn how to think/problem solve ❖ Ability to control impulsivity ❖ Ability to reason ❖ Ability to comprehend ❖ Ability to make decisions ❖ Ability to show personal responsibility ❖ Ability to empathize with others
Embrace diversified learners	❖ To foster an ability to think independently ❖ Ability to think "out of the box" ❖ Schools that focus on graduating students who are critical thinkers

	as opposed to "test takers"
Flexibility for all learners	❖ Early childhood educational foundation ❖ Educational facilities that do not solely focus on standardized tests to determine progress and success ❖ Remove state political influence on textbooks ❖ An education system offering different paths/choices (not just college) and recognizes value/worth of those choices ❖ An education system that is flexible to meet a child where they are ❖ Schools that strive to take into consideration ALL learners when creating curriculum
Cultural and Global Awareness	❖ To build a more civilized society ❖ More learning about the world ❖ To create a better understanding of how the world works ❖ To gain knowledge of other cultures ❖ To create greater understanding and respect between people
Education for all students	❖ Educate all ❖ An education system where results don't vary so dramatically among states ❖ Support for lower income families ❖ To provide equal access to learning to all school-aged kids

> *"The dream begins, most of the time, with a teacher who believes in you, who tugs and pushes and leads you on to the next plateau, sometimes poking you with a sharp stick called truth."*
>
> Dan Rather

Elements of a quality public school education	
Administration	❖ Smaller classrooms and fewer students per teacher ❖ Staff trained on cultural diversity ❖ Culturally competent staff ❖ An educational system that is transparent to parents and the community (its owners) ❖ An education system that is accountable to the community for deliverable results ❖ A system that recognizes criticality of family involvement and support, and finds ways to engage that or provides alternatives ❖ High standards – teachers who are both motivated and capable/competent ❖ Teachers who are trained in sensitivity to broad range of student needs ❖ Support and training for all first year teachers ❖ Provides additional resources for general education teachers about learning disabilities

	❖ School administrators who actively communicate and engage parents in their student's success and continuous growth ❖ Diversity in student population ❖ Rewards teacher performance ❖ Educational support services for kids who need it; community-based needs ❖ Teacher qualifications
Curriculum	❖ What we teach: o Diversity in subjects (science to arts) o Schools that continue to focus on the basics of learning – reading, writing, math, science o Home economics education (how to balance a checkbook) o Unbiased curriculum o Fact-based education o Ability to learn civic responsibilities ❖ How we teach: o Less structure – more hands-on o Teaching how to learn rather than ROTE. Would require different skills/mentality in school system o Education designed to match learning styles; use interest to "light the fire" o To provide opportunities for kids to move forward

	at their own pace o Offer variety of methods in teaching o Recognize and elevate talent of all children
Teachers	❖ Truly dedicated teachers ❖ Models to emulate and follow/great teachers ❖ Teachers open to continuous learning ❖ Teachers who have ongoing commitment to learn and (as needed) change ❖ Guide students with their thinking and not teach to the test
Other Characteristics	❖ Innovation ❖ Advance in technology to promote learning full-time ❖ Less testing ❖ Technology ❖ Real world influence/experiences ❖ Earlier college track awareness ❖ Student portfolios ❖ Post education/recapture older students ❖ Support for parent – to support for children ❖ Summer enrichment ❖ Narrow gaps between economic classes ❖ Investment in school buildings and resources ❖ Provide free breakfast and lunch to all students ❖ Encourage parents to do early childhood education ❖ Extend hours/days

	❖ Interest inventory for students ❖ Affordable child care with education ❖ Parent engagement ❖ Raise center of gravity vs. privilege ❖ Each school district should be measured on its own merit as opposed to comparison to others who are not made up of equal demographics ❖ Summer learning loss

"A child miseducated is a child lost."

John F. Kennedy

"The beautiful thing about learning is nobody can take it away from you."

B.B. King

"Not to know is bad, but not to wish to know is worse."

Nigerian Proverb

What are the barriers to a quality public education and what strategies could decrease these barriers?

Each member responded with five barriers, which were ranked by the group and are presented in order of importance and the barriers in each group received an equal number of votes. Those without any votes are not included below.

Two barriers receive the most support:

- Teacher pay and lack of respect for the teaching profession. Many members said, "When are teachers going to make $100,000/year as they should?"
- Traditional schools models and structures: why K-12?

The next most important barriers are:

- Insufficient funding for public education: money, money, money
- Lack of quality teacher continuing education and staff development
- Difficulties measuring student achievement
- Lack of student investment, motivation, desire to learn
- Family values regarding education
- Insufficient national and state controls
- Criminalization of student behavior and zero tolerance policies on student discipline

These barriers were next considered important:

- JFK ambitions v. no child left behind
- Close-minded elected/appointment government officials

- Organizational inertia: the way we've always done it
- Lack of sensitivity to diversity, learning differences and socio-economic issues

Final barriers in importance:

- Inequality of resources
- Schools don't stimulate curiosity and learning
- Lack of choice of schools (whether by design or geography)

Members briefly discussed strategies that could diminish or end the barriers listed above. The following suggestions were made:

- ➢ Districts should raise salaries to retain teachers, and give teachers more administrative and decision-making authority to improve standing and respect for the teaching profession.
- ➢ To provide greater support for teachers, districts should utilize ongoing professional development, encourage observations of master teachers, require advanced degrees, and provide courses in cultural diversity and multiple intelligence.
- ➢ To encourage innovation, study alternative school models, including tracks that allow students to begin training/employment partnerships or early college programs. Shorten K-12 models by leveraging technology to promote full-time, strength-based learning.
- ➢ Elect public officials who will prioritize education funding and reallocate spending to get rid of unnecessary bureaucracies, such as regional service centers (this is a Texas creation).
- ➢ Broaden types of student assessment, and use conventional tests less often.

- Utilize more creative methodologies and blended learning in the classroom.
- To end criminalization of student behavior and reduce disciplinary issues, teach students to self-monitor and promote self-discipline. Help teachers become trauma-informed and empathetic. Promote understanding of implicit bias. Use restorative justice practices, such as mediation.
- To provide greater consistency across the US, use evidence-based, federally-mandated curriculum and federally-chosen textbooks.
- Amend the US Constitution to grant all children the right to education.

At the close of the session, members were asked the following question:

When you arrived this morning, what did you think about public education and now, after this session, what do you think about public education?

The responses are as follows:

"I used to think this was easy to fix, now, holy cow, it's so much harder and others think the same thing." (Kerri)

"I used to think no one thought about public education and now I realize people really care about it." (Sofia)

"I used to think education was the core of civilization, and that feeling was reaffirmed, in a more complex way." (Joe)

"I used to be naïve about the quality of education in the US, and I was blown away by learning the US is only 17th in global outcomes."(Lynn)

"I used to think only a small group cared about education, and now I realize a much larger group cares." (Joann)

"I used to think education was a simple issue, now I hope I can take this and make a difference." (Claudia)

"I used to think educational policy was done by the elite, now I think all of us have a stake in insuring that we improve education." (Meyer)

"I used to think education was really messed up and couldn't be fixed, now I think there could be more change." (Bobby)

> *"Knowledge – that is, education in its truest sense – is our best protection against unreasoning prejudice, and panic-making fear, whether engendered by special interest, illiberal minorities or panic-stricken leaders."*
>
> Franklin D. Roosevelt

Links to the additional resources used by the group can be found as follows:

"An Overview of the History of Public Education in Texas", Texas Education Agency, located at http://tea.texas.gov/About_TEA/Welcome_and_Overview/An_Overview_of_the_History_of_Public_Education_in_Texas/, Jan. 30, 2017

Stephen Lurie, "Why Doesn't the Constitution Guarantee the Right to Education?" The Atlantic, (Oct. 16, 2013), located at https://www.theatlantic.com/education/archive/2013/10/why-doesnt-the-constitution-guarantee-the-right-to-education/280583/

APPENDIX C – DETROIT, MI

ABA Education Commission Focus Group

Detroit, MI

Notes of 5/5/17 Meeting

Reginald Turner, Clark Hill PLC

Alice Thompson, Hope Academy

Dave Hecker, American Federation of Teachers

Carol Weaver, Detroit Public Schools Community District

Casandra Ulbrich, Michigan State Board of Education

Ivy Bailey, Detroit Federation of Teachers

Shani Penn, Education Achievement Authority of Michigan

Group Demographics:

Gender: 5 females, 2 males

Race: 5 African Americans, 2 Whites

Age: range - 35 to 71 years; mean 53

Occupations: union leader, school board member social worker, education management, teacher, and education attorney

Elements of a Quality Education:

1. Quality teacher in every classroom

a. Consistent, timely professional development for teachers and administrators

b. Giving teachers quality classroom facilities and tools

c. Administrators and support staff focus on supporting the classroom

d. There must be accountability for children to learn to read by 4th grade

2. Understanding and meeting the needs of the families

a. Parental involvement is essential to high quality education, and schools must address the needs of parents in order to educate the children

b. Local, state and federal resources are required to meet those needs and empower schools to help families participate fully in the education of children

c. "Wrap-Around" services including funding for support from NGOs to address needs

d. Quality healthcare (physical and mental) available for all.

e. Discipline programs must be fair, and designed to rehabilitate, not simply to punish – excessive time out of school feeds the prison pipeline.

f. Safety & Security - research-based, state of the art systems should be available to protect the school environment

3. Funding

a. Local, State and Federal revenues should be equal to or greater in urban, high poverty areas. Equity requires more than equality.

b. Where "schools of choice" programs are employed, adequate, accessible, understandable data should be provided.

c. Choice without information is random selection.

d. Adequate resources/facilities for Career and Tech Education

APPENDIX D – EVANSTON, IL

AMERICAN BAR ASSOCIATION | CIVIL RIGHTS AND SOCIAL JUSTICE SECTION | PUBLIC EDUCATION COMMITTEE

MUSKWA CLUB NORTHWESTERN CHAPTER

"NATIONAL RIGHT TO QUALITY EDUCATION" FOCUS GROUP

NORTHWESTERN UNIVERSITY, MAY 28, 2017

Participants: Kim Rowghani- Neuroscience and Psychology student, graduating in 2019.

James Skala- Political Science and Economics student, graduating in 2019

William Whittenbury- Manufacturing and Design Engineering – Moderator, graduating in 2020.

OVERVIEW:

The purpose of this meeting was to provide a college student perspective as part of a national effort by the American Bar Association to ascertain the nature of a theoretical national right to a public education. The discussion group, composed entirely of students, discussed issues facing both higher and primary education and brainstormed possible solutions. The goal of the students was to specifically address education content, and come to a consensus as to what subjects should be made available to every student in the United States. The students hope that this report will aid the ABA in its effort to ensure quality education for all students through the development of a specific and detailed education resolution, which, if passed, will be presented to the government of the United States. This report will include the consensus recommendations, starting with higher education, and include the discussion in italics.

HIGHER EDUCATION- what should be required, and what is the federal government's role in paying for college?

College has become very important in recent years. A college degree is what a high school degree used to be. Currently, high school allows for drop-out even though some education is mandated by all states. A full high school education and at least 2 years of college should be mandated, but an opt-out program should be offered for college for those who would be better served by vocational programs. Rather than offering free college, the federal government should try to maximize the number of degrees earned by ameliorating costs through tax incentives and loan reform (including lower initial costs and refinancing options). The government already requires people to invest in insurance; education should be held to the same importance. Community college should make less of a trade-off between working and going to college; flexible schedules and career support should be offered.

KIM: college is more of a necessity –states mandate education but high school dropout is currently allowed. At least 2 years of college should be mandated.

Opt-out program?

JAMES: College is not free like high school- can gov't force people to pay for college? College should not be made free; rather student debt should be reduced. College loans more affordable and with greater refinancing options down the road. If public colleges were made free, private education would be hurt.

Community college is currently inexpensive.

KIM- some insurance is mandatory- is education on the same level of importance?

JAMES- what is the role of federal government in education? Feds currently don't have control over state condition. States act as testing grounds, benefitting the whole system. Michigan has loose charter schools which are hit and miss. James wants the relationship between federal and state education systems to stay the same. The point of education is social mobility. Fed's goal should be to maximize number of degrees earned by ameliorating costs through tax incentives and loan reform.

KIM- tax incentives are a good point.

K-12 EDUCATION: What are the overarching issues facing K12 education? How do we ensure uniform quality?

America's K-12 system needs more quality control on instruction. We currently have a teacher prestige problem, coupled with low wages. If teachers are valued as much as they are in Finland, for example, public schools would be of higher quality. Contributors to this problem are politically polarizing arguments involving teachers' unions and charter schools.

Standardized tests are still the best way to measure district performance, although they are not perfect. Scores are currently affected by the neighborhood's affluence and how much parents care. Schools should at least be evaluated based on a single national minimum standards test. States should be able to enact more stringent standards if they wish.

JAMES: Quality control on public school systems- getting more teachers into the system. Finland has a high quality public schools because teachers are highly valued.

What is the root cause/solution of the teacher prestige problem?

JAMES: polarized political argument between teachers' unions and soulless charter schools. People get heated over education. High emotional investment from the populace.

People searching for individual solutions that do not help the group as a whole.

KIM: Standardized tests are somewhat necessary to measure district performance. Frequently based on neighborhood and how much parents care. Minimum standard for all school districts set by federal government.

K12 SUBJECT CONTENT:

MATH

GED level math is enough for most vocations. This is all that should be required for students to take, stopping at the current Algebra II level. However, higher-level math is important for some careers, and schools should be mandated to offer higher-level math.

Math- minimum levels Kim and James think GED level math is enough for most vocations. Higher level classes should be mandated to be offered but not required.

KIM- algebra II as the limit- this is what is on the CAHSEE

ENGLISH

In life, good communication skills are more important than math skills. Currently, an upper class bias exists on cultural knowledge- people from affluent areas are more likely to have a richer cultural background. There should be national reading, writing, and speaking proficiency standards. Focus should not be on florid vocabulary, but rather on conveying ideas clearly with correct grammar and strong writing skills. More reading should be conducted in schools, focusing on novels and critical thinking.

English- communication is more important than math in life (Kim). Upper class bias currently exists on cultural knowledge (Kim)

JAMES : ACT vs. SAT – it's good that we have both. ACT is more science focused.

Reading proficiency, writing proficiency, speaking proficiency standards

KIM- focus should not be on fancy vocab- focus should be on conveying ideas with correct grammar.

JAMES: current heavy focus on grammar should shift to writing skills

KIM- more reading, focusing on novels and critical thinking about the novels.

SCIENCE

The most crucial sciences to teach in the schools given the current geopolitical situation is environmental and climate science. Hard sciences including chemistry, biology, and physics should be required, but only at an introductory level. AP-level classes should be mandated for schools to offer but not for students to take.

KIM: earth science, environmental, climate science is

crucial knowledge given the current global situation. Hard sciences- basic chemistry, biology, physics at an intro level (not AP).

HISTORY

There is currently a strong bias in favor of western history in curricula. This causes widespread ignorance of the causes of current geopolitical problems. Curricula also needs to be honest about mistakes made throughout US History rather than sweeping them under a rug. Rather than offering World History, European History, and US History, schools should offer a two class sequence, one on Eastern History (including Africa) and one on Western History (including the US). Both classes should focus on the origins of current events. Hand-in-hand with this, schools should offer more non-western languages as part of their foreign language curriculum.

KIM- history is crucially important, with greater emphasis on non-euro and western history. African and Asian history should be require alongside western/US history. Honest about mistakes made in US history

JAMES- foreign language is part of this.

-more emphasis on non-western languages.

-current event background class- global history.

KIM- we need to include middle eastern history to combat current day prejudice.

JAMES- what is getting replaced with these additions? Do we specialize earlier?

KIM/William- no pigeonholing early

Current events should be tied in to existing

Maybe a western/eastern history instead of US and World

ARTS

Arts should not be required of students, with one exception- music education in elementary school. This program is important because many kids do not otherwise have access to music education opportunities. However, many kids are not artistically-inclined, and should not be forced to take art classes. However, schools should still offer them.

KIM- it's ironic if people are forced to do art. Music requirement in elementary school was really good, because most people don't have other opportunities for music education. But otherwise arts should not be required.

PHYSICAL EDUCATION AND HEALTH

PE should be more informational and educational rather than a physical assessment. Many people simply aren't physically inclined and find it very difficult to pass fitness standards. PE classes do not make a meaningful difference in this area currently. If students are already enrolled in sports, they should not be required to take PE. PE classes should be moved to the end of the day to avoid interfering with academic performance. Health education itself is important but should not be a demanding requirement- it should be less assessment-based and more informational.

In High School, the PE requirement should not exceed 2 years.

KIM- pair it more with health education rather than physical assessment.

Kim- health is important to include in education. Not a demanding requirement- less assessment based, more informational.

JAMES: conflict between sports and PE- if you were doing sports, you got out of PE. Move PE to the end of the day as opposed to the middle. That way it does not interfere with the school day.

KIM: you shouldn't have to do both.

2 years is enough.

STEM

STEM (Science, Technology, Engineering, and Mathematics) is becoming more and more important. High Schools should be mandated to offer introductory-level computer science (with an artificial intelligence focus) and engineering classes, starting at the Middle School level, since students should be able to try out these challenging topics without endangering their all-important GPAs.

KIM: Computer science and intro to engineering should be offered but not mandatory.

Artificial intelligence should be offered as well.

KIM and WILLIAM offer this early- in middle school so people can try it out early without fear of GPA issues.

CIVICS/ECON/GOV/HOME ECONOMICS

Civics classes are very important in today's politically polarized society. This requirement should stay, with heavy emphasis on how people can effect government change individually. Civics classes should also assist students with voter registration.

APPENDIX E – HONOLULU, HI

FINAL REPORT

HAWAI`I'S EDUCATIONAL FOCUS GROUP:

A JOINT PROJECT BY EIH AND THE ABA[3]

January 18, 2017 9:00AM - 2:30 PM

OVERVIEW

Hawai'i's Education System

Hawai`i is unique in the nation as it has a centralized Department of Education (DOE) for the entire state. Area complexes are centered around a particular high school which will then include all middle and elementary schools in that specific district. Thus an area complex could consist of several middle and elementary schools but only one high school.

To understand Hawai`i's education law, one

---

[3]EIH: Education Institute of Hawai`i, a non profit organization; ABA: American Bar Association, a professional organization.

must start with its constitution. Under the Hawai`i constitution, the Board of Education (BOE) is established and empowered as follows:

> ARTICLE X, Section 2 of the Hawaii State Constitution provides for the establishment of a Board of Education.

Section 3 describes the POWER OF THE BOARD OF EDUCATION as follows:

> Section 3. The board of education shall have the power, as provided by law, to formulate *statewide educational policy and appoint the superintendent of education as the chief executive officer of the public school system.* (*emphasis added*) [Am HB 421 (1964) and election Nov 3, 1964; ren and am Const Con 1978 and election Nov 7, 1978; am L 1994, c 272, §15 (HB 3657-94) and election Nov 8, 1994]

The BOE recently released its 3 year strategic plan. In it, the BOE states it has

adopted three policies: E-3, C-3 and 102-15. A copy of the strategic plan is attached.

Policy E-3:

"We believe that our special island home prepares us to lead globally. Our unique values, sense of place, and strong community relationships are increasingly important here and

around the world. In 2015, the BOE approved policy E-3, nā Hopena a'o, or HĀ, to help advance our mission: "HĀ is a framework of outcomes that reflects the Department of Education's core values and beliefs in action throughout the public educational system of Hawai'i. The DOE works together as a system that includes everyone in the broader community to develop the competencies that strengthen a sense of Belonging,

responsibility, Excellence, aloha, total well-being and Hawai'i ("BREATH") in ourselves, students, and others. With a foundation in Hawaiian values, language, culture and history, HĀ reflects the uniqueness of Hawai'i and is meaningful in all places of learning. HĀ supports a holistic learning process with universal appeal and application to guide learners and leaders in the entire school community."

HĀ is being implemented in the DOE through a three-year action plan (2016-2018) developed and led by the Office of Hawaiian Education. Other partner organizations are also adopting HĀ.

Policy C-3:

College, Career and Civic Life has also been adopted by the BOE. The very first goal under Student Success is:

All students demonstrate they are on a path toward success in college, career, and citizenship (C-3 policy).

Policy 102-15:

Policy 102-15 establishes a vision of a Hawai'i public school graduate that states all graduates will:

- Realize their individual goals and aspirations;
- Possess the attitudes, knowledge, and skills necessary to contribute positively and compete in a global society;
- Exercise the rights and responsibilities of citizenship; and

• Pursue postsecondary education and/or careers.

Recent statewide surveys of public school students' aspirations show that 93 percent of all high school juniors hope to pursue additional education or certification.

The BOE Strategic Plan also recognizes the following student outcomes:

GENERAL STUDENT OUTCOMES

Giving back to the community, environment, and world;

Discovering and pursuing their passions so they can reach their full potential;

Demonstrating strong academic and life skills (General Learner outcomes), and showing an ability to think critically, solve problems, and apply knowledge to new situations or contexts;

Being prepared for life after high school, including setting clear goals and developing short-term and long-term engagement in learning;

Exhibiting strength, confidence, and resilience in their everyday lives, and being generally healthy and happy; and

Gaining a strong sense of cultural understanding and appreciation for Hawai'i.

The strategic plan also specifically addressed the achievement gap.

> *Despite an improving economy and low state unemployment, many families continue to struggle financially — more than 50 percent of Hawai'i's public school students are now economically "high needs." Other high-needs students include English Learners and students receiving special education services. In total, 57 percent of students were high needs in 2015. We must also consider the needs of students in ethnic groups that are historically underrepresented in career, college, and community success metrics; it is important to recognize the role of multiculturalism and multilingualism in*

providing a meaningful and equitable education for student achievement. Hawai'i, like many states across the country, continues to struggle with an "achievement gap" that separates the engagement and achievement of high-needs students from that of their non-high-needs peers. It is of the highest priority that schools address the needs of our struggling students.

Funding:

Although there is a weighted formula for each student, not every student receives

an equal amount of funds. Students in more economically challenged areas may actually receive *more* funds than students in the more affluent areas. Funding in the form of impact fees is received from various entities. For example, the military pays impact fees for schools on the respective military bases which the DOE staffs and administers.

Crossroads:

Currently Hawai`i is at a crossroads. The BOE members are now all appointed by the governor as a result of a recent constitutional amendment. The current governor, David Ige, has appointed an ESSA (Every Student Succeeds Act) Task Force which has held meetings statewide with hundreds, if not thousands, of community members including students. The Task Force has produced a draft of the ESSA Plan for Hawai`i in which participants have described their vision for education in Hawai`i's public schools. A copy is attached. In addition, a new school superintendent will be selected shortly.

It is against this backdrop that the Focus Group was convened on January 17, 2017 to answer the following four questions:

Is there a right to a quality education?

Who should receive it?

What are the specifics elements of a quality education?

Who should fund it?

As to the second question, the ten members unanimously agreed that **a quality education must**

start at birth and continue through adulthood. The scientific evidence of the importance of early childhood education is overwhelming. The need to foster community centers of learning at schools for all ages is critical to promoting a quality education.

Smaller groups of three focused on the first and third questions: Is there a right to quality education for all? And how do we define a quality education?

Although the issue of whether there is a constitutional right to education, let alone a quality education, is still unsettled, the Focus Group members believe that because a Board of Education was established by the Hawai`i State Constitution, that **such a right is, at the very least, implied.**

When defining a quality (which definition keeps changing depending on who is in charge) education, Focus Group members noted that one question might be to look at who benefits from a quality education. We believe a quality education should improve society; encourage participation; have an element of empowerment; foster democracy and instill communities with pride. In short, what qualities would we want a human being to have?

We want education to help students develop confidence, self-esteem, "grit," critical thinking skills, problem solving skills, be innovative, collaborative, resilient, joyful, happy, and healthy.

Quality education is when 100% of students are cognitively engaged

and participating. (Not just when one student is answering a question or speaking.) Thus, we believe it is critical that students play an important role in describing their needs and letting them take ownership of their education. And we are not just identifying those students who are the stellar students such as student body officers but we also want to hear from those who are ready to drop out because school does not engage them in any meaningful way.

Focus Group members also ranked the idea of community based education as a priority for creating a quality education. Although communities differ, resources for parents such as literacy programs, job resources, second language learning should be included. In the past, there were vibrant Parent Community Networks in the schools but those have pretty much disappeared. Also there needs to be a recognition that how parents were taught and how students are currently taught differ and thus different learning strategies and techniques are necessary for parents and students.

How do we achieve a quality education?

In addition to identifying the elements of a quality education, our Focus Group looked at what it would take to achieve a quality education. We came up with the following list, not ranked in any particular order:

- Administrators (principals) need to be trained as both managers and leaders; they need to be visible/seen; they need to provide teachers with meaningful evaluations; they need to support teachers and effectively delegate
- Each community should conduct a needs assessment
- Based on the needs, clearly articulated and concrete goals that are strategic, measurable, and attainable should be defined
- Emphasize the importance of the whole child (safety, challenge, engage, healthy and supported; "know every child by name, strength and need"); it is imperative that everyone at school has a safe

environment, one that is free from violence, bullying, discrimination, and drugs

- Two kinds of staff: those that teach and those that support the teaching
- Teachers must be trained and qualified in specific content; teachers need to be recruited and supported (Many teachers are recruited from the mainland but not given the tools or social network to make the adjustment to Hawai`i's culture)
- Reorganize or restructure administrative systems to support schools, teachers and students
- Foster partnerships with community resources for schools (Hana School, Waipahu High School, Kaiser High School are all amazing examples of schools with tremendous community support)
- Sufficient funding to lower class sizes; fully fund schools with teachers adequately paid
- Array of support for teachers from the community, the Department of Education, and principals that allows for transfer of discipline responsibility from teachers to administrators, supports teacher innovation, consistent mentorship
- Curriculum that is fun and engaging for students, students engage with each other and work together to complete interactive tasks, learning related to student's life
- Students involved in choosing curriculum; students actively engaged in their

education, and students having a stake and ownership of their education
- Teaching students "common good", civic mission, service learning through involvement in the community, and to be informed citizens [mentioned by two groups]
- Availability of co-curricular activities
- Community involvement; schools to actively involve and engage their communities
- Whole child education that includes global competencies
- Early Learning and Pre-K that is affordable and available
- Maximizing the opportunities available in the Every Student Succeeds Act (ESSA)
- Remove barriers to allow schools to go as far as they want to provide the best education for their students, encourage the "wide open field" instead of erecting barriers (example: one middle school had community support to build an auditorium but was told that the DOE policy prohibited auditoriums in middle schools)
- Power of ongoing self-evaluation of and by all stakeholders
- Resources for technology and environmental awareness and sustainability

Our Focus Group also looked at specific ways to achieve the quality education given Hawai`i's unique structure:

- Revise the Department of Education structure that defines schools or complex areas as independent Learning Education Agency (LEA) to allow them to be incubators of innovation
- State legislature and Board of Education should adopt a policy of right to quality education

GROUP SUMMARY REGARDING FUNDING

Finally our Focus Group looked at the following funding questions:

Who should receive it?

- Revise Charter school funding formula and rules
- Schools

Who should fund education?

- Non-profit and charitable organizations
- Federal government
- State government
- Parents, residents, tax payers
- Businesses
- Military

How should it be funded?

- Taxes & Impact Fees: real estate development tax, marijuana tax, tourism related taxes

- Crowd-funding
- Lottery
- Community support: Schools themselves also need to improve public relations and marketing strategies to increase direct contributions from the community – improve branding and messaging, increase visibility, and build relationships

Members:

6 Women

4 Men

Age: 30 to 60+

Occupations represented:

Former politician, author, Education Commission member

Owner of a small publishing press

Retired judge, author, educator

Outreach coordinator with a non-profit organization

Former elementary school teacher (now attorney)

Former attorney (now involved with charter schools)

Art educator

District administrator

Educational specialist for the judiciary

Executive director of a history center

APPENDIX F- JACKSONVILL, FL.

Right to Quality Education Focus Group

Partnership for Child Health
(partnershipforchildhealth.org)

Jacksonville, FL November 2016

Elements of a Right to Public Education:

1. Sustained and equal funding
    a. Every school should have the financial resources to provide all necessary tools and instructors to meet the educational needs of students and faculty.
    b. This would address disparities in student access to textbooks, internet, and optimum learning environments.
    c. Pay for teachers should be increased taking their educational attainment, performance and proficiency targets, student and peer feedback, adherence to continuing education, and other qualitative markers into account – none being dispositive individually. Teachers should also be consulted and help determine what a nation-wide standard for pay should be (adjusted for location/standard of living and tied to inflation).

2. High Quality Instruction
    a. There should be a standardized teaching curriculum that every teacher shares.
    b. Like doctors and lawyers, teachers should be licensed and have minimum continuing education requirements.
    c. Education should include child socio-emotional development, classroom management, childhood development, etc.

3. Adaptable/Responsive/Positive Learning Environments
    a. Students learn and apply themselves differently. Some students will go to college. High quality education should be responsive to the needs and abilities of the individual students and should include vocational tracks, alternatives to standardized education (that is strengths-based and purposeful).
        i. This would counter-balance current trends to teach to tests.
    b. All educational tracks and institutions should be championed so as not to preference or negatively message public, private, vocational, or ESE programs or institutions, as well as to highlight the equally important avenues for student educational attainment.
    c. Institute Positive Behavioral Interventions and Support (PBIS) to focus on changing *environments* instead of the person.

4. The Whole Child

   a. Education does not exist in a vacuum. Neither are the experiences of students, faculty or staff isolated from their personal lives.
   b. Like colleges, schools should be one-stop shops: medical, mental health, dentists, and necessary goods should be available on-site, including, where necessary, access to child care.
   c. Focus on life skills, play, arts, and music should return to schools.
   d. Adopt rights/Equity-based approaches to learning and school environments, discipline and planning (see below).

5. Student Voice and Participation
   a. Age-appropriate student feedback and input into the environment, curriculum, teacher performance, policies, and functioning of the school environment is critical to creating a sense of ownership and belonging for students. Meaningful expression of their voice and participation acknowledges their rights and ability to contribute to the educational environment. It also increases their understanding of their responsibilities to the school environment, and the multiple factors that go into ensuring a quality education and experience not just for them, but for their peers, teachers, and staff.
   b. Rights-Respecting Schools recognize the interdependent, indivisible rights of all children, and acknowledges that a child

cannot have their right to education fulfilled without their right to nutrition, pleasure and play, freedom from violence or exploitation, access to information, or right to safety to name a few.

6. Community Messaging and Engagement
   a. Frameworks – like Jacksonville did for children's mental health, engage Frameworks (and/or marketing/PR professionals) to develop strategies to understand how the community thinks about education and public education, and development values, frames and metaphors that redirect negative or fatalistic assumptions or beliefs. The entire community should use these new frames, metaphors and shared values statement to reframe the discussion about education, optimal delivery, positive environments (and discipline), and how we measure success
   b. Engage public-private partnerships to increase funding for schools, economic development in surrounding school communities and offer students opportunities for professional internships and apprenticeships (banking, law, medicine, aeronautics, nursing, cosmetology,

Demographic info:

2 nurses

1 lawyer

1 foster care utilization specialist

1 baker act utilization specialist

1 grant management administrator

2 black females

2 white females

2 black males

Age range 25 - 43

APPENDIX G – LOS ANGELES, CA

1/23/09

Los Angeles County, South Bay, Right to Quality Education Focus Group - Findings

Background

Our focus group consists of eight men and women with diverse ethnic, cultural, professional and economic backgrounds. Our group consists of African Americans, Asian Americans, Latino Americans, Caucasian Americans, current educators, retired educators, the executive director of an education related foundation, a school board member, an engineer/parent, and a lawyer/parent. We met every few weeks over the course of four months. First, we worked to identify the issues we saw in education today. Then, we gathered broader input from our various constituencies. Finally, we put together a document we feel summarizes our findings with respect to those elements most needed to foster a quality education.

The following summary is meant to provide a spring board from which to develop specific initiatives that the ABA or other concerned entities can advocate both regionally and at a national, congressional level.

Core Elements of a Quality Education Program

We believe that every child should receive an education which prepares him or her to become a successful, contributing member of society. To ensure that each child receives such an education, certain basic standards should be established nationwide, and each child should be tracked throughout his or her educational journey so that no individual loses his or her right to proceed and succeed through our educational system due to varying standards based on different venues.

Based on feedback from a survey of Human Resources Professionals and our personal relevant experience, we believe that every child is entitled to an educational program which includes, at the very minimum, proficiency in the following skill sets and abilities by the end of high school: (Note: we have endeavored to list the following skill sets in order of greatest importance)

1The ability to read at an eighth grade level.

a. If it is determined that a child has fallen behind his or her expected grade level at any evaluation period prior to the end of each grade level, the educational institution should apply early intervention methods designed to advance the child toward his or her grade level expectations.
b. Such academic evaluations should be performed no less than twice per school year, beginning no later than the start of first grade.
c. Interventions can also commence on teacher recommendation.

   d. Thoughts on cost free intervention strategies are discussed in the section immediately following "Core Elements".
2. Basic English Grammar and Writing Skills
   a. The ability to define and use basic sentence structure
   b. The ability to write a coherent paragraph with a topic sentence
   c. The ability to write a business letter
   d. The ability to write a basic essay with a thesis sentence and concluding paragraph
   e. The ability to spell or use spell check
   f. The difference between different forms of words which sound the same ie. too, two, to
3. The ability to execute basic mathematical tasks including the following:
   a. Addition and subtraction
   b. Multiplication and long division
   c. Use and manipulation of fractions (add/subtract, multiply/divide, reduce etc)
   d. Use and manipulation of percentages (similar to "c" directly above)
   e. Basic applied geometry (shapes, angles, distances)
   f. Basic statistical analysis. (averages, means, medians, etc.)
4. Basic accounting skills and economic knowledge including:
   a. Balancing a checkbook
   b. Creating and maintaining a budget
   c. Using a calculator or equivalent
   d. Understanding the effects of leverage, interest rates, and compounding

   e. Basic macroeconomics: national debt/deficit, GDP, balance of trade, tariffs, free-trade, cost of labor, and the importance of education when competing in the labor market
5. The ability to communicate and cooperate effectively with others including:
   a. Listening skills
   b. Public speaking
   c. Debate and reasoning skills
   d. Conflict resolution skills
   e. Personal responsibility
   f. Ethics
   g. Character development
   h. Etiquette/manners
6. US Government and Judicial System
   a. State vs. Federal
   b. Constitution, statutes and common law
   c. The electoral process and the role of elected officials
   d. How do judges get/keep their jobs and what is their job?
   e. Civil vs. criminal actions
   f. The balance of powers
   g. What is a democracy and why is it our choice?
   h. Other types of governments and how they differ from ours
7. National and World Geography
   a. The locations, names and capitals of each US state
   b. The continents and large demographic areas within them (i.e., Europe, Middle East, Asia)
   c. Trading partners

   d. Raw materials, industries, or technologies indigenous to certain regions (diamonds, coal, oil, etc.)

8. US and World History

   Note: we recommend teaching history in order to demonstrate to students elements such as cause-and-effect, consequences, and conflict resolution through real-world examples. To achieve this goal, we would not necessarily encourage students to memorize volumes of historical dates, names and facts, but more importantly, focus students on gaining functional wisdom and knowledge designed to equip them to make informed social/political decisions, elect representatives, and utilize the electoral process in the best interest of our country. Examples of such lessons would include, but are not limited to:

   a. Why our Civil War and the two World Wars were fought.
   b. What caused changes within certain countries' political systems
   c. Major social, technological or economic progressions that drastically changed society and how they changed it. (Industrial Revolution, Internet, etc.)

9. Graphical communications (reading maps, road signs, assembly instructions, diagrams, etc.)
10. Science
    a. The principles of momentum, inertia, gravity and other forces

b. The earth relative to the solar system, galaxy and universe
c. Basic chemical reactions
d. Different sources of energy and how they are created
e. Physical Earth Science in terms of avoiding or understanding the potential for natural disasters
f. Health
    i. Proper exercise
    ii. Proper Nutrition
    iii. Living your life according to healthy choices

11. An Introduction to extra-curricular opportunities
    a. Theater
    b. Dance
    c. Music
    d. Art
    e. Sports
    f. Vocational Opportunities (wood shop, welding, mechanics, cooking, sewing, etc.)

Intervention Strategies

We strongly support early intervention where class work, teacher observations, or test scores indicate a need for immediate improvement. Not all interventions must result in additional funding requirements.

For example, such interventions could consist of:

1- One-on-one, peer to peer tutoring/mentoring.

a. Harness student strengths and raise self-esteem by allowing students proficient in one subject to help students struggling in that subject.
b. Do not limit the opportunity to be a tutor to those proficient in all subjects. For example, allow a student to tutor math and receive tutoring in language.

2-Senior Adult to Child Tutoring/Mentoring

a. By establishing a School Mentor Corps, schools could access a steady stream of youth and senior adult tutors/mentors via a volunteer and a scholastic credit program.
    1. For security purposes, each tutor/mentor should be checked by Megan's law; finger printed and photographed.
    2. The program could access senior adults by means of a referral network among

the families at the school, public advertisement, and utilizing already known retired professionals from the school system.

3. The program could draw on their own senior youth in the school - adding to school spirit. Student mentors could receive scholastic credit and a recognition award upon graduation in return for tutoring/mentoring.
4. Tutoring/mentoring preparation could include a 4 hour training class with the principal, covering rules of conduct, emergency response, etc.
5. We recommend that once a week each child meet

with his or her tutor simply to be affirmed and encouraged in any academic concept and/or challenging element in his or her school/life experience.

b. We also suggest a big brother/sister program in order to minimize the need for intervention.

Alternative Education Opportunities:

Based on our research and relevant experience, we believe that educational institutions should provide optional 'skilled-labor' educational opportunities, in addition to the required traditional 'academic' education. The determination as to whether a student should participate in the alternative education program should be made collaboratively between the student, the parental guardian(s), and the educational staff. The objective of offering alternative opportunities is to allow the student to choose the educational path which best maximizes his or her overall future well-being, self-satisfaction, and long-term productive assimilation into society.

Students who choose to participate in the alternative education program may need to have a modified 'academic' curriculum to account for time and resources allocated to alternative education. When determining modifications to traditional class requirements, we recommend preserving, as much as possible, the core elements listed above.

This focus group sees that the most important forms of alternative education to provide are vocational shops and apprenticeships where students learn both practical and marketable skills and trades. If possible, students should be paid for doing productive work in order to discourage a student from dropping out from school to pursue low-wage alternatives. A paid apprenticeship allows the student to develop professional skills, making them more marketable in society, and at the same time allows the student to stay in school to attain the traditional academic education.

This method has proved successful at the Cristo Rey Schools, among others. Please see article, *ABA Journal,* Jan. 2009, p. 11. *Fortune,* Dec. 8, 2008, p. 115

Parental Involvement:

The educational institution should encourage parental participation in the student's educational experience. This includes actively recruiting and encouraging parents to participate in PTA meetings, co-op programs, and field trips. The administration should urge parents to communicate regularly with teachers and school administrators, especially concerning sub-par homework or test performance, behavior problems, or emotional problems. The administration should work collaboratively with other community organizations such churches, athletic leagues, relevant governmental agencies and truancy programs to encourage parental participation. Where the teacher or administration feels a child is truly at risk, such teachers and/or administrators should feel free to visit the parents if they cannot get the parents to come to them. See www.CSMonitor.com/littlebillclinton for an excellent series: "A School Year in the Life of a New American" which demonstrates the importance of schools interfacing with the parents and the community.

Enforcement:

We should hold Federal, State, and school district agencies accountable for any practice which would result in disadvantaging highly mobile students or students who lack parental support of their educational objectives. For example the evaluation and enforcement criterion for school districts should eliminate any incentives to leave a child behind a grade, pass a non-deserving child, or allow a child to drop out of school. District assessment criteria should penalize administrators who allow such undesirable things to happen. Conversely, the evaluation criteria should reward efforts to help a problem student stay enrolled and improve academically – even if the student's performance is below par. Administrations should never benefit by disadvantaging a student and should always benefit by doing the very most they can for each individual student. If a child is having trouble in school, teachers and administrators are encouraged to meet with the child's parents in their home, at school, or in a safe and inviting place to work as partners with the child's parents or guardians towards the child's success. When a child moves between districts both the outgoing and incoming district should be held responsible for making the child's transition seamless according to the basic core standards outlined above. The child's file should be sent within one week of receipt of a request from a new District, and the incoming District should give credit for all work completed toward the national standard established.

Further possible programs and incentives:

A National Corp of Senior Mentors should be established to provide guidance, support, and tutoring to those students who lack family support. Schools should offer parenting classes. Schools should receive extra dollars for each child enrolled who is in foster care. Those dollars should help provide extended library hours after school and mentors to help guide and support these children. School Administrators should focus on supporting teachers to do the best job possible.

The importance of mentors for disenfranchised children cannot be overlooked. Several groups have demonstrated the importance of mentors in helping disadvantaged children succeed. Some such groups include LA Challenge and the South Central Gifted Scholars Fund.

As our society moves more toward technologically advanced production, the need for more math and science teachers grows. The use of scholarships and fellowships has proven effective in attracting those successful in the math or science to the teaching profession. See "Wanted: More science and math teachers" by Stacy Teicher Khadaroo, *Christian Science Monitor*, Monday, December 29, 2008 at 3.

Further, all areas of academics can prosper from good teachers. We believe good teachers not only achieve good results on standardized tests, but incorporate enthusiasm, and creative teaching methods into their classrooms. Many people, who have achieved success in their chosen profession outside education, reach a point where they would like to give their knowledge to students in a classroom environment. While certain basic teaching skills are requisite in the classroom, a five year degree may not be necessary for those with other college degrees and many years' experience in a different profession. Therefore, we encourage the development of guidelines for teacher certification which would open doors for individuals to change careers and teach what they have been doing for many years in practice.

Although we have endeavored to propose intervention programs with minimal fiscal impact, we recognize that if the Federal Government mandates any programs related to education that would have a potential fiscal impact on school districts, those programs must then be fully funded by the Federal Government.

Comparisons of the American System of Education with Those of Asia

We must not forget that many foreigners come to the U.S. for a better education. It appears to our focus group that people in America have more freedom or choices (i.e. in the university) in terms of what they want to learn in U.S. than in Asia. The advantage of this is that children can make their own decisions on what they really want to study in the U.S. On the other hand, the advantage of the education system in Asia is that children have more discipline, and they have more support from society. We do not feel that Asia offers a better educational program to children and then U.S. However, we believe that there are many core elements which help children to complete or succeed in their education in Asia that may be lacking here such as:

(1) Support from Social workers
(2) Support from family members (parents, grandparents, relatives.)
(3) Support from the school or teachers (who really care about the students, make phone calls to the students' home or visit the parents on their own spare time)

(4) Commercials made by the government to guide or lead children toward making the right decisions for their future.
(5) After school programs
(6) Night school programs
(7) Financial Aid

In addition, Asian education provides or puts more emphasis on art, music and exercise than do American schools.

How to Handle a Student's Re-entry to School after a Previous Drop Out

We believe that all people should have the right to a basic education as outlined though the core elements enumerated above. Therefore, even if a child drops out through their own actions or due to circumstances beyond their control, they should have the right to resume their education to that standard at any time in their life. To that end, community colleges should maintain a program designed for that purpose. Although a thorough examination of such programs was beyond the scope of our focus group to date, we feel that the California Community Colleges come close to offering a model for such a program.

Students should be allowed to resume their education with similarly situated peers to reduce the embarrassment of returning to school after an extended absence. Again, internship programs integrated with academics can increase the incentive to return to school. Please note that we do not believe that students should be paid merely to attend school. However, when a person contributes valuable work, his or her work should be valued in order to establish self-esteem, marketable skills, and life-sustaining income.

Respectfully submitted,

Talley Allen

Tim Battle

Nini Battle

Ju Wei Chen

Rolex Montoya

Thelma Whidden

Garry Whidden

Beth K. Whittenbury

Randy Winston

Appendix A

Summary of the Basic Skills Polled HR Professionals Listed as Necessary for Entry Level Positions[4]

Academic Skills:

1. Ability to put a coherent sentence together
2. Ability to understand how a paragraph works
3. Ability to spell as well as understand and recognize common words with different spellings (e.g.: "their" vs. "there")
4. Ability to communicate in standard, professional English.
5. Ability to read, retain and comprehend basic instructions
6. Ability to manage basic computations – addition, subtraction, multiplication, and division (and fractions).
7. Use of proper grammar in speech and writing
8. Basic Geography (countries, continents, which countries are in which continents, oceans, seas, equator)
9. Legible handwriting

Basic Life Skills:

---

[4] Informal poll of Professionals in Human Resources Association Members (PIHRA, a southern California Chapter of the Society of Human Resources Management "SHRM") using the general list-serve conducted on Nov. 14, 2008 and summarized by Beth Whittenbury.

1. Knowing how to speak with colleagues and clients in a professional way (e.g.: no "dude", "whatever", etc. in the conversation)
2. Understanding how work and personal relationships are not the same
3. Understanding and practicing excellent customer service.
4. Understanding that the boss is the boss and if you don't agree, you don't get a "timeout" or get to complain to another authority – this is a workplace, not home or a classroom.
5. Basic Phone Etiquette
6. Critical thinking skills (being able to read, retain and apply what's read to situations which differ from those examples given in the text.
7. Understanding that gossip and rumors will not be tolerated in the workplace.
8. Taking Responsibility
9. Understanding and exercising duty and honor
10. Understanding that a job pays you for your work, not based on your financial need or any sense of entitlement
11. Speaking without use of slang, the ability to clearly articulate oneself.

Legal/Civics/Economics Skills:

1. Understanding the basic problems with workplace romance

2. Understanding the basics of how a business runs and what's important and what's not.
3. Business Ethics
4. Understanding the workplace
5. Knowledge of which legal documents workers need to provide to employers
6. Knowledge of legally allowed interview questions
7. Understanding how our government works
8. Understanding of our court system
9. Understanding of how G8 countries operate their governments
10. Understanding why civil and world wars were fought
11. Basic finance skills – income vs. expense, budgeting, how to balance a checkbook and the need to do so, 401K and other retirement planning options, the necessity of living within one's means, responsible use of credit/leveraging
12. Understanding the rights of others in a business environment
13. Conflict resolution skills

Practical Skills:

1. Computer and typing skills (be able to use basic excel and word software)
2. How to dress appropriately
3. How to interview
4. Timeliness

5. Proper handshakes
6. Use of eye contact
7. Use of the spell check and grammar check features
8. The importance of providing accurate information
9. The use of professional layouts
10. Knowledge of how to prepare a resume
11. Respect in the workplace
12. Refraining from personal errands/business while at work
13. Willingness to learn
14. Understanding that an employee has a responsibility to his or her employer
15. Understanding that professional/work relationships are not the same as personal relationship and how to keep them separate

Appendix B

Results of Informal Poll of Parents and Students in a Predominately Latino Community

"The teachers have to like teaching and not just go for a paycheck."

Need a person just to help with discipline in the classroom in addition to the teacher.

Need more history and science.

Needs to be more discipline in High School. Kids need to stay in the classroom and not cut classes.

Smaller class sizes. No more than 15. This is for High Schools.

“There was no Dean of Students (disciplinarian) in my High School.”

“When a kid wants to drop out, he’ll drop out.” So, schools need to make it harder to drop out.

“They need tutoring classes. Don’t give them a choice to drop out.”

There has to be special programs for kids who want to drop out or who are at risk or who don’t want to follow rules. All employers should make a High School Diploma a requirement to get a job. That way, parents can’t force kids to work instead of finishing school and kids don’t think they have an alternative.

Those kids who are doing bad at school, make him part of school. Give him something to do to help at school, like tutor others in something he understands. Don’t isolate those that make trouble; bring them into the fold.

“The main thing is not to give kids a choice to drop out.”

APPENDIX H –OKLAHOMA CITY, OK

Focus Group on Right to Quality Education
Oklahoma City, OK
Facilitator: Jennifer Marshall, LCSW

Group Demographics:

- **Gender**: 5 females, 2 Males
- **Race/Ethnicity**: 4 white, 2 black, 1 Hispanic
- **Age**: range - 29-63yrs; mean - 45yrs
- **Occupations:** social work, early intervention home visitation program, education, health care, administration and research

Elements of a Quality Education:

1. **Whole-Child Approach**
    - **a.** Academic progress can only be made when the physical and social-emotional needs of students are made a priority (Maslow's Hierarchy of Needs)
    - **b.** This approach will require more student supports in the school, with *at least* a nurse, social worker, and school counselor in every school building
    - **c.** Social-Emotional Learning curriculum should be included as a necessary component of the student learning process
    - **d.** Schools should provide multiple pathways to "success", meeting the needs of the entire spectrum of learners

   e. Restorative Justice should be used as a framework for correcting student misconduct, limiting out-of-classroom time to address behaviors
2. **Full-Service School Approach**
   a. Utilizes a Community School-based system
   b. Meets the needs of that particular student body/community, decreasing the one-size-fits-all-schools requirements
   c. Schools partner with community resources (health care, mental health, food pantries, etc.) to meet identified needs
   d. Promotes full-staff teamwork to meet student needs, from custodial staff to office staff to teaching staff, etc.
3. **Schools should reflect the Culture of the Community in which it serves**
   a. Defining the "culture of the community" is deeper than race and ethnicity and should include the system of beliefs, values, and assumptions about life that guide behavior and are shared by a group of people.
   b. Districts should promote collaboration with those systems of influence in the community
4. **Equal Funding that is based on more than test scores**
   a. How well a school/district is performing should be evaluated by other factors such

as health and wellness, SEL assessments, and academic growth

   b. Schools should be given more freedom in decisions regarding the use of funds and should involve community input

5. **Value Student Voice**
   a. Student-needs should drive policy/approach
   b. Promote accountability system within the student body, recognizing the positive power of group influence
   c. Invite former students back into the school in the form of internships and mentorships
   d. Recognition that students know what they need; educators need to be willing to ask, listen, and respond

APPENDIX I – ORLANDO, FL.

AMERICAN BAR ASSOCIATION CIVIL RIGHTS AND SOCIAL JUSTICE'S SECTION EDUCATION COMMITTEE

Right to Education Focus Group Results
Orlando, Florida
Facilitator: Deshaud Brunson, Law Student

Introduction

Education is essential for the exercise of all other human rights because it promotes individual freedom and empowerment. Education is a powerful tool that has the ability to lift adults and children out of poverty, and it allows individuals to become productive members in their respective societies. Speaking with a group of passionate students and administrators at Florida A&M College Law there were two main discourses: (1) Education should be established as a fundamental right on a national level, and (2) there should be a right to education, a quality education.

Brown v. Board of Education marked a huge victory for the great Thurgood Marshall, civil rights activist, and young children across the globe. In the world changing opinion delivered by Chief Justice Warren, "We conclude that in the field of public education the doctrine of 'separate but equal' has no place. Separate educational facilities are inherently unequal." *Brown v. Board of Ed. of Topeka, Shawnee County, Kan.*, 347 U.S. 483, 495 (U.S. 1954). Decades after the Brown v. Board decision, the United States still struggles with providing education to all. Thurgood Marshall's victory gave the

United States a great start, but there is still much work to be done.

The focus group determined that education should not only be a fundamental right in the United States, but also the education afforded should be of sufficient quality. UNICEF describes a quality education as, "content [that] refers to the intended and taught curriculum of schools. National goals for education, and outcome statements that translate those goals into measurable objectives, should provide the starting point for the development and implementation of curriculum." https://www.unicef.org/education/files/QualityEducation.PDF(UNICEF, 2000).

Background

This report summarizes focus group findings conducted as part of the ABA Civil Rights and Social Justice Section's Education Committee. The findings are based on a focus group that was conducted around the state of Florida, specifically in Orlando, FL. The focus group explored people's experiences with education and the ways in which their cultural beliefs and values were, or were not, incorporated throughout the educational system.

The focus group was conducted by a culturally mixed group consisting of African Americans, Latino Americans, Caucasian Americans, Asian Americans, Youth, and LGBTQ (lesbian, gay, bi-sexual, transgender, and queer) individuals; in addition, this group consist of parents, educators, advocates, and education consumers within the United States. Ages range from 23 to 59.

The Method

At the inception of the focus group, participants were first asked a general question, "should education be established as a fundamental right in the United States? And, if so, how far should that right extend?" This two part question yielded passionate responses that have been recorded in this report. Ultimately, those findings led us to a discussion on the quality of education.

Results

1. **Education should be established as a fundamental right on a national level, and the education received should be of sufficient quality.**
   - After establishing that education should be a fundamental right, the focus group determined that education must be of substantial quality. In order for the quality of education to be satisfactory the group stated a list of factors that would define what a quality education was.
     - Students must be healthy (well-nourished), (2) students must be in a safe environment, (3) Students must have well trained educators, (4) students must be trained in literacy (not trained to take a test) and (5) students must have relevant standard-based curriculums structures and adequate literacy materials (no outdated books).
       See https://www.unicef.org/education/files/QualityEducation.PDF. This list records everything that the focus

thought should be provided for a quality education to be sufficient.

1. Students must be healthy both mentally and physically.
    - Students with disabilities have to have a better support system and well-trained teachers. Students with disabilities should be able to reach basic literacy levels when they graduate high school.
2. Students should be in an environment safe from bullies.
    - Former Educator, David Johnson, stressed the importance of providing a safe environments for students as well as focusing on the well-nourishment of students in public school. He stated, "A lot of these students do not eat before they come to school, and some do not have food at home when they leave the school."
3. Students must have access to qualified educators, and educators have to be paid for their service.
    - "I cannot blame the educators! The great educators pay for their own materials, my great grandmother was an educator in the 1950's & 60's who, like most educators in the public schools today, paid for her own teaching material." – Deshaud Brunson
4. Students must not be trained to take standardized test, but rather a national exam should be given to access the schools progress with students.
    - In order to evaluate or test the quality of our education some students want to implement

a national exam. "My thoughts on the current education system as a whole is that there needs to be a national exam instead of State standardized exams. It is already well known that when it comes to Math and Science, the United States as a whole ranks far lower than we should . . . to continue making up as many end of the year placements exams . . . does not help the process. I believe national exams will allow all of the teachers in different states to be on the same page." - Rebekah Knight

5. Students must have a standard curriculum that is not focused on passing a test. Students need to be taught to be more productive as a society before graduating high school. This includes learning how to be an informed voters and write checks.
    - "We have been taught to prioritize a return of investor dollars rather than the benefit to society as a whole. The first priority of our education dollars should be the growth and development of our society, not investor profits. By making the benefits to society our main priority, we can focus on innovation and opportunity as the return on our investment." – Bill Ramos
    - "When public schooling first started our society was quite different. Post elementary schooling was largely superfluous. Outside of basic reading, writing, and arithmetic, school was only needed if you were to become a scholar. Contemporary society is much different.

> In contemporary society, you can not apply to most minimum wage jobs without a high school diploma." - Michael Scott

Funding

- The schools should be funded on a national level
- Property taxes provide support for most of the funding that local government use to fund education.
- Local governments collect taxes from both residential and commercial properties as a direct revenue source for their local school districts. Wealthier property localities have the ability to collect more in property taxes and poorer communities with smaller property tax base will raise less funding to support the local school districts. This can often mean that children that live in low-income communities with the highest needs go to schools with the least amount of resources.
- In Florida, the average district spends $9,231 per student. According to the National Center for Education Statistics (NCES) 11,011 per student, so Florida spends $2,000 less than the nationwide average. https://nces.ed.gov/fastfacts/display.asp?id=66. These numbers are shocking; however, even with some states like Florida grossly underfunding public schools the United States still spends more than other developed nations on its students' education each year. Although we spend more the U.S. still trails behind a lot of other developed nations. Thus, adequate funding alone cannot produce quality education.

- In the words of President Lyndon Johnson, "Poverty must not be a bar to learning, and learning must offer an escape from poverty."

In conclusion, everyone has a right to education. It is the corner stone of a civil society, and everyone disserves to have a quality education.

Focus Group Members:
Michael Scott (Mike Scott), Former Educator & Law Student
William Ramos, U.S.M.C. Veteran & Law Student
David Johnson, Former Educator & Law Student
Rebekah Knight, Law Student
Kyle Jones, Law Student
Deshaud Brunson, Law Student
Florida A&M Law Library Staff

APPENDIX J –PALOS VERDES, CA

Right to Education Focus Group

Facilitator: Krista Galleberg

Palos Verdes Estates, CA

Who:

Our focus group met on Tuesday, January 12 and Thursday, January 14 for three hours each. The first day we had 10 members; the second day we had nine members (eight returning members and one new member). In total, our group consisted of four men and seven women. Our youngest member was 18; our oldest member was 89. The remaining nine members were roughly between the ages of 40 and 70. Eight members were Caucasian; one was born in Iran; one was born in Morocco; one was born in the Philippines. All are permanent residents or citizens of the United States. Participants had varying degrees of familiarity with the American public education system. Two are currently employed as full-time public school teachers; three others have had teaching experience. Other occupations represented: founder of a successful marketing/social media company, real estate agent, elder care, homemaker, student, business consultant, engineer.

What:

Our focus group agreed that all children residing in the United States have a right to a quality education. A quality education is an education that helps students develop their own interests/abilities and prepares them to survive as adults in our society.

How: *Note that the following section is primarily about logistics and probably does not belong in a constitutional amendment. The amendment should make a claim about justice and opportunity, not about specific infrastructure, academic subjects or skills. That being said, our policy suggestions are as follows:*

Minimum academic standards We agreed that the following skills would mark an able student who received a quality education. This is the national minimum for curricula designed by the states for able students:

- Literacy (reading and writing in English)
- Numeracy (general math skills, such as adding, subtracting, multiplying, dividing, percentages, basic personal finance, etc.)
- Communication skills (sufficiently effective oral and written communication)
- Basic understanding of technology and science
- Exposure to personal care strategies (consequences in decision-making, nutrition, sexual health, interpersonal relationships, exercise, etc.)
- Introduction to extracurricular/creative activities (art, music, etc.)

Disabled students There should be a national basic minimum standard for all able students as noted above.

Our group acknowledged that not all students in the United States would be capable of meeting a minimum threshold of skills, no matter how low that threshold is. However, these disabled students still have a right to a quality education. Therefore, there should not be a "one-size-fits-all" definition of a quality education.

Learning environment There should also be a national basic minimum for school conditions. These conditions are related to the right to a quality education but distinct from the minimum threshold for state curriculum. School conditions include:

- Children must have their basic needs met while at school. If they don't, they cannot learn. Basic needs are:
    - Nutritious food
    - Safety
    - Emotional and psychological support
- Children must have at least one hour per day to do their homework in a safe space with adequate supplies (e.g. Computers, tutors) and adult supervision
- Children must have qualified teachers at all times during their education

Curriculum development States should continue to set their own standards and are encouraged to rise above the national minimum.

Accreditation The government (either, state, federal, or a combination) should take steps to oversee school accreditation in ways that will minimize bias and controversy in school evaluations.

The definition of a successful school must depend partly on local factors. However, all schools must meet the national minimums outlined above in order to become accredited.

Intervention and Enforcement If a school fails to be accredited, both the state and the federal government should provide resources to help the school improve itself. These interventions must operate in a culture of mutual trust and cooperation. The goal of an intervention is to get the school back on the right path as quickly as possible, and then leave the school leadership to govern itself.

Resources to help failing schools may include:

- Funding
- Team working on behalf of the accreditors: This team should consist of educators who have been successful in a similar environment to the school deemed "failing", as well as university professors and school personnel from around the state or country. Solutions must be developed in collaboration with existing school leadership and on a case-by-case basis.
- Team working on behalf of the school: Corps of community members (paid or volunteer) to give the school the manpower it needs to become accredited (fill out forms, assemble/file paperwork, etc.)

Accountability Accountability measures (oversight, school turn-around, etc.) must foster success, not punish failure. Reform policies must be team-oriented and proactive.

Public school organization

- Developmentally-appropriate activities at all ages in school (especially important during the younger years)
- Early education for children aged 2 and 3
  - Optional
  - Government-subsidized based on income
- Pre-K for children aged 4
  - Optional
  - Free for all children (I.e. No tuition)
- Kindergarten through grade 10: one track
  - Mandatory
  - Free for all children (I.e. no tuition)
  - Expose all children to different options: a wide range of academics (math, science, language, art, music, etc.) as well as a wide range of vocational options (coding/tech, plumbing, carpentry, mechanical, etc.)
  - Help students find what they like doing
- Grades 11 and 12: different tracking options; students track themselves with guidance from adults
  - Optional
  - Free for all children (I.e. No tuition)
  - Vocational track: heavy on vocational training, limited academic training still available
  - Academic track: heavy on academic

    - training, limited vocational training still available

- Higher education
    - Optional
    - We did not discuss who should pay, etc. because we did not consider higher education to be part of the bare minimum for a quality education

Role of the federal government The Department of Education should have some role in public education. At the bare minimum, it should be able to ensure that states are not falling below the national minimum threshold for curriculum standards or school conditions. Perhaps, the proper role of the federal government is to check the power of the states and protect districts from being overpowered by the states.

Note We discussed home schooling briefly, but didn't address it for this document. We did not discuss online education.

Signed,

Cindy Damon

Krista Galleberg

Soraya Greenway

FatemmehNamvar

Rob Perry

Judy Seitelman

Lily Seitelman

Bingoo Villanueva

Steve Wells

(Our last member wished to remain anonymous)

APPENDIX K – ST. LOUIS, MO

Right to Education Focus Group
Facilitator: Val Hirschberg
Saint Louis, MO

Who:

Our focus group met on Wednesday, May 10th for two and a half hours. We had 7 members present, and one facilitator. In total, our group consisted of 3 women and 4 men. Our youngest member was 18; our oldest member was 23, all members were undergraduate students at Washington University in St. Louis.

Five members were Caucasian, three of which were children of immigrants (one with parents from Russia, one with parents from Greece, one with parents from Canada); one member was African-American and one was Filipino. All participants are permanent residents or citizens of the United States. When not at school in St. Louis, three live in Los Angeles, one in Chicago, one in Philadelphia, one in St. Louis, and one in New Jersey. Participants represented a wide range of socio-economic backgrounds with participants self-identifying as lower, middle, upper-middle, and upper class.

Participants had varying degrees of familiarity with the American public education system and legal system- one participant is studying education, while another was pre-law. Other participants are studying marketing, economics, French, mathematics, and one was pre-Med. All had attended high school in the United States- 4 went to public school, 2 went to private school and 1went to a boarding school.

What: I first prompted the group by asking if there should be a federal right to a quality education?

The focus group agreed that all children residing in the United States have a right to a quality education through 12th grade. Our group defined a quality education as an education that provides access to tangible resources (books, clean buildings, quality teachers) and intangible resources (human capital, networks). Lastly our focus group defined a quality education as an education that prepares students to live as adults in our society. This right should extend to anyone in the student age population in the United States – regardless of citizenship.

Note: While the group defined access to these "intangible resources" as part of the right to quality education- this idea was not fully developed in the remainder of their discussion.

How: Next, I prompted the group discussion by asking what a right to quality education means in practice to them? And what should a right to a quality education include? After about 2 hours of discussing these are the conclusions they came to:

Minimum academic standards The focus group agreed that the following skills would mark an able student who received a quality education.

- Literacy (reading and writing in English)
- Numeracy (proficiency in basic arithmetic and financial literacy)
- Basic understanding of how to use technology (ability to type, navigate the internet)
- Informative health and wellness classes that teach

healthy eating, stress management and mental health care, sexual and reproductive health, general strategies for healthy living.

Disabled students The focus group acknowledged that not all may be capable of meeting a minimum academic standards, due to potential physical or mental disabilities. They decided that these students still have the right to a quality education. They agreed that this means students with disabilities have a right to teachers that have specific credentials and training in special education.

Vocational Schooling The focus group agreed that not all students may be looking to pursue a college degree or any form of higher education. As a result, they agreed that students should have an option starting in 10th grade to opt into a vocational school that provides technical training.

Learning Environment Conditions My focus group agreed that there should be a national standards for school " learning environment" conditions. This seemed to be the focus groups catch-all group in which they lumped a variety of aspects they perceive as integral to the legal right to a quality education and an adequate learning environment. These conditions, according the group, include:

- A classroom, and school environment, that meets some basic standard of cleanliness (i.e.
no mold or other hazards, clean/fresh air, potable drinking water, sanitary bathrooms and lunchrooms).
- Free nutritional breakfast and lunch for all students.
- Free afterschool care (providing time to do

homework, games, snacks)

- A minimum standard of school supplies and resources- including up to date computers, text-books, white boards, and any necessary instructional equipment.
- Access to quality teachers (see accreditation and teacher training below)
- Access to elective courses (especially in the creative arts).
- Access to outdoor recreation and organized sports.
- A classroom environment of no more than 20 students (The group deemed a class size larger "realistically unmanageable and inevitably unequal").

Accreditation and Teacher Training The group decided that students have a right to quality trained teachers. They agreed that there should be a national standard of teacher quality and wanted to see the best state level teacher-training program adopted as a national standard. (Some group members expressed that ideally teachers should be required to have a masters in education to teach).

Funding Our focus group agreed that included in the right to a quality education is the right to a adequately funded education. Our group agreed that funding of schools should be equitable and adjusted depending on location (i.e the cost of resources, facilities, food, etc. may differ from city to city and should be adjusted to account for these differences). While many focus group members were not familiar with how school funding currently works, they expressed concerns about the inequity of school funding and agreed that they wanted to ensure that students have a

right to an adequately funded education.

Final Notes

- We briefly discussed higher education, yet it was not a substantial portion of what our focus group perceived to be a part of a federal right to quality education.
- Lastly, in the beginning of our groups discussion, one member started one of her ideas with the phrase "In my perfect and ideal world" which prompted a short discussion among group members as to whether the wanted the rest of their discussion regarding the right to quality education to be realistic and feasible, or idealistic. They decided not to focus on feasibility (and agreed that this was not in the scope of their knowledge base) and instead focused on their ideal scenario of what a quality education would look like.
- Group members wished to remain anonymous in this report.

Signed,

Valerie Hirschberg

APPENDIX L – WASHINGTON D.C.

AMERICAN BAR ASSOCIATION
CIVIL RIGHTS AND SOCIAL JUSTICE SECTION
PUBLIC EDUCATION COMMITTEE

'National Right to Quality Education' Focus Group Washington, D.C.
June 29, 2016
6:00-7:30PM

OVERVIEW

Purpose: The ABA Civil Rights and Social Justice Section's Public Education Committee is seeking input from parents, teachers, principals, school administrators, policymakers, advocates, and advocates on the creation of a definition for the 'National Right to Quality Education in America' and what it should look like.

While there have been a few discussions in the past on what a constitutional amendment on the 'right to education' should entail, the Section's Public Education Committee is vested in gathering pertinent information that will not only be memorialized, but can be actualized through future collective advocacy efforts.

The Section's Public Education Committee is currently collecting feedback from education consumers and providers in other states and would like to ensure the District of Columbia has a voice in the process as well.

Process: The participants would first identify the

issues involved in creating a quality education for all - what barriers do students, parents, teachers, school practitioners, et. al face? Then, the discussion would move to what specific elements should be considered necessary to a quality education (e.g. who should fund it; should it apply to Pre-K through Grade 12 or K-Grade 8; should it be limited to math and reading; what general protections are we seeking to create in the amendment, etc.).

Goal/Outcome: The Section's Public Education Committee hopes that the findings will support the development of a comprehensive plan and proposed ABA resolution that, if passed, can be part of the ABA's larger advocacy efforts before Congress, the Executive Branch and other governmental entities.

D.C. Focus Group Members:

- Cathy Reilly, education advocate
- Laura Fuchs, teacher
- Ruth Wattenberg, state board of education member
- Maria Blauer, education attorney
- Patrice Wedderburn, education attorney
- Ayan Islam, law student

SUMMARY

The focus group meeting opened up with an overview of the state of education in the United States in contrast to international counterparts. In addition, there was a review of a resourceful website - www.constituteproject.org, which contains numerous constitutions from different countries and each topic can be filtered to determine how many countries have the 'right to education' embedded in their constitution.

After the overview of the purpose of the focus group in contrast to national statistics and global constitutional models, the focus group participants raised key points around the need to develop a state-by-state strategy since there are approximately 45 states that provide either a constitutional or statutory 'right to education.' As a result of the discussion, it was noted how the District of Columbia (D.C.) does not have the 'right to public education' in any of its statutes and may need guidance in drafting legislation that promotes the 'right to education' and/or a section that can be incorporated into a revised draft of D.C.'s proposed constitution.

The dialogue contrasted the issues between the national right to education vs. local right to education, the historical and current educational topics that are impacting D.C., and the current politics that is raising the question: what is next in D.C.'s education system? Two sets of recommendations resulted, with each tackling the 'right to public education' from a local/state perspective.

MEETING NOTES

• Overview of D.C.'s laws – compulsory attendance (which doesn't equal to equitable educational access).

• Federal disability laws serves as a powerful vehicle with ensuring students are protected, receive equitable access, and receive an affirmative right because of the laws and funds attached to associated programs.

• Discussed the rhetoric that ensued during the push for the UN Convention on Persons with Disabilities and how the matter was misinterpreted.

o The convention was viewed as an attack on family rights/decision-making and there were concerns that the convention would both degrade the sovereignty of the U.S. plus parent's ability to freely homeschool.

Framing the right to education must be universally palatable and should not be viewed as an attack on any subgroup.

• Why not look at housing or health? Equally as important in retaining/supporting communities.

o Different ABA Section committees have different directives and are tackling that issue.

• The attempts to nationalize were unsuccessful but yielded gains when done on a state-by-state level, especially since it impacts state discretionary spending and is the largest in state budgets.

• Discussion on San Antonio v. Rodriguez and the measuring stick in Abbott v. Burke.

o Funding is an issue that needs to be resolved.

o San Antonio v. Rodriguez.

In this case, respondents brought a class action on behalf of parents and students residing in poor school districts in Texas, alleging the State's system of funding schools based on local property taxes denies equal protection to students in poor districts.

This has created a situation where education was deemed not to be a fundamental right.

• As a barrier towards quality education and equitable funding, it was suggested that San Antonio v. Rodriguez be re-litigated to remove this impediment towards equitable access to quality education.

o Abbott v. Burke.

In this New Jersey case, schools in the Abbott district were not equitably funded due to an unfunded statutory mandate that violated the state's constitutional guarantee that all communities, even the poorest, receive "thorough and efficient" system of education.

The class action-lawsuit of 20 families from the cities of Camden, East Orange, Irvington, and Jersey City resulted in universal preschool, K-12, and supplemental or at-risk program funding reforms as well as school-by-school reform of curriculum and instruction.

Noted as a good example of a class action lawsuit with an end goal and a realistic/achievable yardstick.

• Note: Important because some lawsuits have not been effective in achieving the requisite outcomes for children and families.

• Community engagement

o Since D.C. does not have any 'right to education' provisions, perhaps a town hall or campaign to educate residents will force everyone to look at the 200 schools, the empty seats in both public and public charter schools, and question the very capitalistic markets that are driving both sectors to determine – what should be done in the best interest of our children/students?

This will raise a number of interesting questions and spur a conversation on what D.C. or a state should provide.

• Helpful to get everyone thinking about current systems, e.g. IMPACT (teacher evaluation system).

• What shall we cover as a right? D.C. constituents will have to wrestle with its own notions of 'right to education' before trying to figure out what it should be on a national scale.

o E.g. How to reduce mobility between students transferring schools mid-year or out of state.

o How to effectively use taxpayer funds? o What do parents want?

E.g. when D.C. Council passed special education (SPED) reform laws, which hadn't happened for years, it was due to a councilmember's political advantage to do so. Otherwise, SPED students would not have had affirmative rights outside of federal laws. Thus, political timing matters.

Current issues in D.C. highlight the need for an education advocate.

o Questions surround how to frame the discussion, whether it's legislative or constitutional and make the discussion raise the public's conscious.

• Constant tension between the feds/states and maintaining state sovereignty (e.g. Common Core). o Better to attack the issue via states since its been acknowledged that there are 45 states which have the 'right to education' in their constitutions or statutes.

o Let states expand the right to education on their own. Each community has distinct needs and issues that can be addressed in the local/state level.

o Also, states panic whenever there's a question or idea about further federalizing a program or increasing the federal government's role. E.g. Common Core was a prime example on the attempt to create a standardized national education, and how it was rebuffed by many states.

• Equity is at the core point of the issue.

o A question was also raised about schools getting closed and children losing access to education, which also raises an issue on equitable access to quality education.

- Definition of standards and goals o How do we define quality education?
  Is it physical space?
  Class size?
  Resources? Research-based?
  Learning and output
  What does quality mean? Might have different meaning to different groups.
  o What goals are we seeking?
  E.g. In the Blackmon-Jones lawsuit, the original goal was to create more inclusive classrooms and instead the result was a database and process. o How do we get the public to realize education is a civil rights issue?
  o What are the outputs?
  E.g. measuring based on PARCC results?
  Creation of productive citizens
  Are results actually reflective of reality?
  o How much control will a school or school district have?
  o What are the inputs?
  Where will the money go?
  What other programs will supplement a child's education? Arts, music, sports, etc. o Develop standards that are catered to local/state systems.
  Language should be broad not loaded that it threatens/undermines local rights.
  Language should be crafted in a ways that the public can galvanize around.

- How do we preserve parents and citizens' rights to have the same level of agency within the system? o E.g., parents and public are constantly being removed from what is conveyed as a democratic, decision-making process. Since D.C. officials are working on a November ballot referendum on D.C. statehood, there were interesting points made regarding the lack of authenticity within the democratic process with attaining resident input on the proposed D.C. constitution.

- o A number of advocates are upset that the D.C. Council and drafters of the constitution did not add a sentence regarding the right to education.
  - Also didn't help that the federal bill of rights is, allegedly, being adopted wholesale for D.C.'s draft bill of rights and the 2nd Amendment is being included only to appease Congress while it is against the will/interests of the residents.

- Is the current system following a democratic process?
  - o Issues need to be viewed from democratic rights, process perspective.
  - o Is the local system truly democratic?
    - How are decisions being made versus the decisions that have been already made?
- Sometimes community meetings were held to share finalized rather than solicit ideas.
  - o How about the school board? Is it a democratic process from election to constituent advocacy?
    - Clearly a need for elected school boards and a mention of existing research that validate the need.
    - Also, what happens to student outcomes if there isn't democracy in our school boards?
  - o How can we measure engagement and if the

system is democratic?

o Due to the currently complicated makeup of governance in the education system, there are more problems created than solved.

E.g. in D.C., the school board does not have the same authority as others in most jurisdictions, and there are constantly differing opinions between policymakers and legislators on what their respective roles/responsibilities should be.

- We have a Chancellor that oversees a large school district (DC Public Schools = 1 Local Education Agency (LEA)) and reports directly to the Mayor;
- 62 public charter school districts that are overseen by the Public Charter School Board (an independent authority created by Congress);
- A Superintendent of D.C.'s state education agency, which oversees federal compliance and grants management; and
- A Deputy Mayor of Education who oversees citywide education strategy and education-related agencies.

As a result of the confusing governance structure, data has been reported in differing formats, and issues still persist with reducing the achievement gap due to competing bodies with competing policies and missions.

A discussion should be had about roles and responsibilities, especially with regard to rulemaking authority and process.

- Perhaps a third party, such as the ABA, hosts a town hall that will galvanize the community to think about D.C.'s education system. o It'll remove the matter from key players and allow the public to decide.

o Perhaps such third party can support states or provide states guidance on how to develop good governance structures for community input.

- Maybe helpful to have a concise document that displays each state's 'right to education' section and what D.C. should consider for their constitution proposal. o Include best practices on democracy and effective representation.

- National civil rights change on an issue always occurred on a state-by-state basis. The same strategy should be considered for education.

RECOMMENDATION

As a result of current, local politics surrounding the proposed D.C. statehood constitution and the lack of a transparent, democratic civic engagement process, the participants in the room shared how they would prefer to see (if possible) support from the ABA on strategies towards attaining good governance and democratic representation in relation to school boards and executive and/or legislative branch advocacy (especially due to our unique political system).

The two recommendations are:

- **Develop and introduce a study that assesses the 45 states' 'right to education' constitutional language or statutes**. Study can highlight if the education codes are currently effective, has it been watered down (law/constitutional right not being implemented effectively or at all), and more. Once the study is complete, the ABA can: o Host a panel discussion or town hall introducing the study so the remaining jurisdictions, like D.C. know what the key points are in order to draft their own educational rights and to assess what efforts should be made in states with deficient implementation of educational rights.

- Conduct a campaign using model 'right to education' statutes as a means of educating and effectuating change.

- **Conduct town halls that assist communities on forming their own 'rights to education' statutes or constitutional amendments.**
  Host town halls in D.C. and remaining states to engage and guide communities on what does the 'right to education' look like and provide guidance/strategies on how organizations can lobby for such changes with their legislative bodies to develop a local/state standard that is broad enough and does not threaten local rights.
  - Note: Maybe by having all states with the 'right to education' on the books, the ABA can then move for a larger national right or it might be easier to get states to ratify the Convention on the Rights of the Child and even the Convention on the Rights of Persons with Disabilities.

SHARED RESOURCES

• International Education Index http://thelearningcurve.pearson.com/index/index-ranking/overallscore-highest

• Why Doesn't the Constitution Guarantee the Right to Education http://www.theatlantic.com/education/archive/2013/10/why-doesntthe-constitution-guarantee-the-right-to-education/280583/

• Database of Country Constitution's https://www.constituteproject.org/search?lang=en&key=edfree

APPENDIX M - ABA RESOLUTION 117B ADVOCATING ESTABLISHMENT OF VOTING CURRICULUM

AMERICAN BAR ASSOCIATION

COMMISSION ON THE LAWYER'S ROLE IN ASSURING EVERY CHILD'S RIGHT TO A HIGH-QUALITY EDUCATION
SECTION OF CIVIL RIGHTS AND SOCIAL JUSTICE
COMMISSION ON YOUTH AT RISK
STANDING COMMITTEE ON ELECTION LAW
CENTER FOR CHILDREN AND THE LAW

REPORT TO THE HOUSE OF DELEGATES

RESOLUTION

RESOLVED, That the American Bar Association urges federal, state, local, territorial, and tribal governments to develop and implement age-appropriate curricula designed to instill in all students a sense of personal responsibility to cast informed votes and to teach them how to educate themselves regarding candidates and issues in elections.

REPORT

The American Bar Association (ABA) has long encouraged measures to instill or enhance civics education in our schools, including public education about the justice system and rule of law in our society. Specifically, in Resolution 114 (1995) , the ABA committed its support to public education to foster understanding of the Constitution and the rights and responsibilities of citizenship as fundamental to the continued functioning of our democracy, and urged the legal profession to engage the support of policy makers to further this goal through implementation and support of civics education in elementary and secondary schools.

Our citizens become eligible to vote as they leave the secondary school system. Consequently, schools generally have not focused on preparing students for something they can't do until they graduate. However, the primary and secondary levels of education should be where our students learn about democratic processes fundamental to their continued wellbeing. Although engaged Parent, Teacher Student Associations (PTAs) often stage mock elections for students or take a few, privileged students on state legislative lobbying trips, no uniform effort is made to teach our students the importance of voting and how to educate themselves as to candidates' backgrounds, positions, and qualifications as well as the facts underlying ballot propositions and other issues.

The goal of this resolution is consistent with Justice David Souter's keynote speech during the 2009 Opening Assembly of the ABA Annual Meeting in Chicago, in which he said, "I believe civic educational reform is, literally, essential to the continued vitality of American Constitutional government as we know it." In response to Justice Souter's call to action, then ABA President-elect, Stephen Zack, wrote: "We must rededicate ourselves to learning about our constitutional system . . . We must begin where the need is most urgent and the impact can be the greatest – in our nation's schools."

Under the "Goals 2000: EDUCATE AMERICA ACT ((P.L. 103-227)" enacted in 1994, Goal 3, which was to be achieved by the year 2000, was: "3. STUDENT ACHIEVEMENT AND CITIZENSHIP: By the year 2000, ail students will leave grades 4, 8 and 12 having demonstrated competency over challenging subject matter including English, mathematics, science, foreign languages, civics and government, economics, arts, history, and geography, and every school in America will ensure that all students learn to use their minds well, so they may be prepared for responsible citizenship, . . ." (emphasis added). It would seem hard to contemplate a student prepared for responsible citizenship who doesn't understand the need to vote and who does not know how to find the facts relevant to key issues in any given election. Yet, the proliferation of "fake news" and personal viewpoints vented through social media makes training on how to filter out all but genuine facts relating to key issues especially critical. The U.S. has one of the lowest voting participation rates among western democracies. This fact further supports the need for passage of this resolution.

The American Bar Association has long supported efforts to increase voter participation, in fact the predecessor entity to the Standing Committee on Election Law was a Special Committee on Election Law and Voter Participation. The proposed resolution fits squarely with long standing Association efforts and policies to encourage voter participation by lawyers (Standing Committee on Election Law, August 1989) and college students (Special Committee on election law and Voter Participation and the Young Lawyers Division, August 1972). Most recently, the Standing

Committee on Election Law has partnered with the Division for Public Education to create resources for the purpose of educating secondary school students about the process and importance of voting (http://www.americanbar.org/groups/public_services/election_law/voting_electionlaw_resources.html). The Standing Committee and the Division developed a video encouraging students to vote (http://youtu.be/NLHnzi3lWUM) and the Standing Committee also created a website www.voteyourvoicenow.org which includes information about voter registration and voting for each state and territory.

In the words of the Standing Committee on Public Education in its 1995 Recommendation and Report to the House of Delegates (#114), "The timeliness of such support is critical to a renewed commitment and understanding of the fundamental relationship between rights, responsibilities, and the rule of law in preparing young people for effective citizenship." Twenty-two years later, we must take stronger, more targeted steps to ensuring our citizens receive the tools they need to actively and effectively fulfill their civic duty to vote in all elections.

Respectfully submitted,

Reginald M. Turner
Chair, ABA Commission on the Lawyer's Role in Assuring Every Child's Right to a High-Quality Education

August 2017

BIBLIOGRAPHY

Why Doesn't the Constitution Guarantee the Right to Education?:Every country that outperforms the U.S. has a constitutional or statutory commitment to this right., by Stephen Lurie, Oct. 16, 2013, see at https://www.theatlantic.com/education/archive/2013/10/why-doesnt-the-constitution-guarantee-the-right-to-education/280583/ (last visited 7/30/2017)

https://www.unicef.org/education/files/QualityEducation.PDF UNICEF, 2000).

Fania E. Davis, 8 Tips for Schools Interested in Restorative Justice, Sept. 26, 2014, found at https://www.edutopia.org/blog/restorative-justice-tips-for-schools-fania-davis. Last visited 7/30/2017.

William Haft, More Than Zero: The Cost of Zero Tolerance and the Case for Restorative Justice in Schools, 77 Denv. U. L. Rev. 795 (1999-2000).

Made in the USA
Monee, IL
04 November 2026

67388672R00095